Praise for *My Life After Death*

· ·

"This book is unique in that it describes what existence is like for Erik Medhus *after* his physical death. It is interesting to envision Erik's mode of communication with 'living' loved ones—and to contemplate the various realms and experiences described as he becomes aware of his true nature. But I most appreciate his fresh take on the value of Earth life, reflected by these words: 'Hold hands, man. Hug everybody. Have a hugfest.'"

—Mark Ireland, author of *Soul Shift* and *Messages from the Afterlife*

"Communicating through a medium, Erik Medhus draws us into experiencing his world and his life in the afterlife. We experience his senses, emotions, thoughts, amazement, discoveries, and surprises as he has lived them since his passing. *My Life After Death* is an absorbing journey through the afterlife that I recommend to anyone who wants to understand the realm we will all eventually inhabit by experiencing it through the engrossing accounts of this young man living there now."

—R. Craig Hogan, PhD, author of *Your Eternal Self*

"From the graphic description of finding himself looking at his own dead body and seeing all the commotion and heartache that his suicide caused, Erik Medhus provides us with a totally new perspective on what it's like to die. His voice is clear, direct, and intimate as if talking to a close friend in the language of young people today. His insights are poignant and profound. Erik tells it like it is, no punches pulled."

—Dr. Victor Zammit, coauthor of *The Friday Afterlife Report* and *A Lawyer Presents the Evidence for the Afterlife*

Praise for *My Son and the Afterlife*

"Dr. Elisa Medhus offers a heartfelt, deeply moving story that invites readers to question their own beliefs of love, loss, and the afterlife."

—Eben Alexander, MD, author of
the *New York Times* bestseller *Proof of Heaven*

"Elisa's journey has been amazing, and she is well qualified to share her knowledge with both the medical community and the grief community. She . . . is breaking new ground and leading the way for many of us working in the field of bereavement, hospice care, and consciousness."

—Terri Daniel, author, educator, end-of-life advisor, interfaith chaplaincy, and founder/director of the Afterlife Education Foundation and the Annual Afterlife Awareness Conference

"*My Son and the Afterlife* is a book that will tug at your heart strings and make you laugh, cry, and more importantly, consider possibilities that you have probably never thought about before."

—Thomas Campbell, physicist and author of
My Big TOE (Theory of Everything)

My Life *after* Death

A MEMOIR FROM HEAVEN

Erik Medhus
with Elisa Medhus, MD

ATRIA PAPERBACK
New York London Toronto Sydney New Delhi

BEYOND WORDS
Hillsboro, Oregon

ATRIA PARERBACK
An Imprint of of Simon & Schuster, Inc.
1230 Avenue of the Americas
New York, NY 10020

BEYOND WORDS
20827 N.W. Cornell Road, Suite 500
Hillsboro, Oregon 97124-9808
503-531-8700 / 503-531-8773 fax
www.beyondword.com

Managing editor: Lindsay S. Brown
Editors: Emily Han and Sylvia Spratt
Copyeditor: Henry Covey
Proofreader: Jade Chan
Design: Devon Smith
Composition: William H. Brunson Typography Services

First Atria Paperback/Beyond Words trade paperback edition September 2015

ATRIA PAPERBACK and colophon are trademarks of Simon & Schuster, Inc. Beyond Words Publishing is an imprint of Simon & Schuster, Inc., and the Beyond Words logo is a registered trademark of Beyond Words Publishing, Inc.

For more information about special discounts for bulk purchases, please contact Simon & Schuster Special Sales at 1-866-506-1949 or business@simonandschuster.com.

The Simon & Schuster Speakers Bureau can bring authors to your live event. For more information or to book an event, contact the Simon & Schuster Speakers Bureau at 1-866-248-3049 or visit our website at www.simonspeakers.com.

Manufactured in the United States of America

10 9 8 7 6 5 4 3 2 1

Library of Congress Cataloging-in-Publication Data

Medhus, Erik, (Spirit).
   My life after death : a memoir from heaven / Erik Medhus with Elisa Medhus, MD.
      pages   cm
   1. Spirit writings.   2. Future, life.   3. Spiritualism.   I. Medhus, Elisa.   II. Title.
   BF1301.M53   2015
   133.9'3—dc23
                                                          2015013069

ISBN 978-1-58270-560-6
ISBN 978-1-5011-0472-5 (eBook)

The corporate mission of Beyond Words Publishing, Inc.: *Inspire to Integrity*

To my daughter Kristina Braly.

. . . .

I am so profoundly grateful to you for creating the *Channeling Erik* blog. If you hadn't, I would not have begun my journey from darkness to light; Erik's death would have been a tragic waste; and he and I would not have had the platform from which to help others the world over. In no small measure, you have saved my life and your brother's too.

A Note

· ·

Suicide Is Never the Answer

Having lost my son to suicide, I would hate to see anyone go through the same pain that I had to and still, to some degree, endure. If you suffer from depression and have any thoughts of suicide, please seek the help of a mental health professional and rely on the support of all those in your life who care for you and can help you. If you are contemplating suicide, please call the National Suicide Prevention Lifeline at 800-273-8255, and remember that suicide is a permanent solution for a temporary problem.

Contents

Part IV: My Life Today

Foreword

....

by Elisa Medhus

Erik Rune Medhus came quietly into this world at three o'clock in the afternoon without so much as a whimper. He gazed around the room as if in awe of this new place where he would live for all too brief a period of time. When our eyes locked, the chemistry was palpable. I knew he would be a bright light in my life.

As a child, Erik was so well behaved, often playing with his Legos quietly in his room while his siblings were running roughshod nearby. Even when he was only eighteen months old, he demonstrated a tremendous capacity for compassion. I remember the day I brought him home from the pediatrician's office after he'd gotten a slew of childhood immunizations. His thighs were littered with Band-Aids, and his cheeks were stained with tears. My husband, Rune, asked him how his day had gone, and with his head resting on my shoulder, he said, "I have a good time." He didn't want us to worry about him. In fact, he frequently wanted to console us. Whenever I held and comforted him after he got a boo-boo, he'd pat me on the shoulder as if to comfort me.

Erik grew up in a home in a Houston neighborhood with my four other children, Rune, and me, so our family was big and boisterous. There was never a dull moment in our energetic and playful household. Erik, third in the pecking order, was the mischief maker among his siblings. He loved playing practical jokes on them and often teased them with a sense of impish delight. His siblings weren't the only ones who were a target of his pranks, though. He'd often hide behind the kitchen cabinets and then jump out and yell, "Boo!" when Rune or I came home from work.

Playtime with his siblings was always creative and frequently noisy. One of his favorite games was to chase them through the house with his tighty-whities on his head while pelting them with rolled-up socks. He also loved playing war outside with his brother and sisters and some of the neighborhood kids, toting airsoft guns around and in full camouflage clothing and face paint.

Erik had a beautiful mix of softness and toughness to him. He loved all things beautiful—especially women. He even asked his preschool teacher for her hand in marriage. He also loved anything with wheels, just like his father did. For that reason, Erik looked up to Pappa, a stockbroker by trade, and wanted so badly to be a part of his world of fast cars and faster motorcycles.

As for the two of us, our relationship was very close. In fact, we could share anything with one another, and Erik had no qualms about discussing what other children would consider inappropriate dialogue with a parent. He even asked for advice about sex. I cherished that closeness and was amazed at his candidness and trust.

Despite his happy start, Erik changed around the time he became fourteen. He suffered from severe bipolar disorder—an illness that can turn terminal. The light within him began to lose its glow as he entered his teens, and life here on Earth became extremely difficult for him.

Ours is an affectionate and caring family. Not a phone call ends or one of us leaves without an "I love you," and there's never a shortage of hugs to go around. As with all my kids, nearly every night after our ritual of bedtime songs and stories I would tell Erik how grateful I was to have him in my life, and I'd recount all the things I thought were special about him. Erik had his good days, but even medication, therapy, and the closeness of our family failed to coax him from that dark place he tumbled into, where misery became his near-constant companion. Because of his mental illness, his moods would frequently plummet to the deepest depths of despair. He'd sleep often in an effort to escape the pall cast over him. When he was awake, he was often sullen and quick to anger. Conflict and drama became a familiar part of our family's life.

Erik tried to appease his demons through immediate gratification. Maybe a new hobby would bring him a brief period of joy. Maybe a new bike. Maybe a new skateboard. These things never gave him the lasting happiness he sought; instead, they only brought brief glints of sunlight before being washed away by the relentless rain of bipolar disorder. In addition, Erik suffered from learning differences and odd motor and verbal tics. Because of these, he was often the target of bullies—not only his peers but in some cases his teachers too.

His "friends" would let him down frequently, saying one thing yet doing another, breaking one promise after another, pretending to care and then talking about him behind his back. Sometimes they'd invite him over to "chill" but then leave before he got there. I was often the sad witness to their cruelty. I remember sitting with him outside one day, listening as he called his friends one by one only to have them pick up the phone and then hang up.

In spite of how he was treated, Erik never hurled a personal insult at anyone. Sure, he got angry or disappointed, but he never tried to tear a person down by calling them names. And though his gift for compassion often went unrecognized, it never faded. He was always there for a distressed friend in need. He made himself completely available, saying things like, "I'm here for you. Do you want me to come over and sit with you?" And I'm sure that when he did sit with that friend, he listened well.

Strangers seemed to gravitate toward Erik. I don't know why. Maybe they, too, sensed the good in him like we all did. People used to approach him at our local Starbucks, where he liked to hang out and bum cigarettes, and they'd share their stories with Erik as he listened patiently and lovingly. When one of these newfound lost souls started to cry, as they often did, he would wrap him or her in a warm embrace and say, "Look, dude, you're coming home with me. My mom's going to make you a home-cooked meal." I made many unplanned trips to the market, but it was always worth it.

Erik was also very open and candid. His conversations were peppered with his usual sailor talk and honesty—a sincerity that made him easily approachable. To him, words were just a string of letters; they got their power from the intent behind them, and his intent was always pure and positive.

As a mother, watching his suffering was agonizing. It seemed like nothing I did helped, and I tried everything. I mean *everything*. Nothing done or said could soothe his pain. All I could do was watch from the sidelines, my broken heart in my hands, witnessing his illness slowly sap the life from him.

Just after his twentieth birthday, Erik died from a self-inflicted gunshot wound to the head.

This book is the memoir of my son Erik, who in his own words shares his journey into the afterlife from the moment of his untimely death to the present, giving a glimpse of what's to come for all of us. Knowing he "survived" his death and now thrives in a new dimension gives all of us, at the very least, pause and, at the very most, comfort, enlightenment, and inspiration.

As painful as it was to witness and as painful as it still sometimes is for me to relive some of these experiences, they have also been an opportunity for immense healing and growth. I'm very proud of what

Erik's doing in his role as a spirit guide, giving so much to so many people throughout the world, often saving lives not only figuratively but literally too. I had to dig deep to find the courage and strength to continue after Erik's passing, but I know now that although it comes at a heavy price, I was meant to share my son with the world.

Erik communicates with me largely through spirit translators. With their help, Erik has shared all he knows about death, the afterlife, his life as a spirit, and more. All this is recounted in my first book, *My Son and the Afterlife: Conversations from the Other Side*, which also chronicles my arduous journey from a skeptical physician who was raised by two atheists to a believer without so much as a shred of doubt.

This book is more about his journey than mine. Through the translation of gifted spirit translator Jamie Butler, Erik tells his story of life after death in a way that heals on many fronts. For instance, it is truly amazing to watch Erik heal himself through his own words as he processes and shares his experiences on each page. He has evolved and grown up as he's found his footing in his new home and discovered his own worth in a way that he never could when he was "alive."

Erik's words have also healed my entire family. We now know he's not gone forever but lives on with a renewed sense of joy and purpose. We see that he's no longer miserable like he was here on Earth. And because of him, spirituality has become an integral part of our family's life and beliefs. We now realize that the soul survives death and that we are eternal beings here to grow and expand from our human experience.

It is Erik's hope that his words will help demystify death by helping us shed some of the fear and dread surrounding it that so many of us experience. By shining a bright flashlight into that dark and mysterious forest of the unknown, he brings to anyone who will eventually die—that is to say, everyone—both insight and comfort, along with the will to live life as it's meant to be lived: out from underneath the shroud of our own mortality.

Through Erik's words, love, and joy, our relationship has changed. It's better. Richer. Deeper. We "talk" more than we ever have before, but our conversations don't just revolve around his misery. They take a larger stage, delving into topics that are meant not only to change my life and my family's but those of people across the globe as well. Although our loving relationship has reached new heights, I know that it will continue to grow and strengthen even more, because love knows no boundaries—not even death.

Erik, Mama loves you forever.

A Note from Erik Medhus

··

Hey, I'm Erik. Yeah, the dead guy. Weird, right? Trust me, I get it. It took me a while to get used to it too. I'm not a zombie (although I guess that would be kind of awesome), and I'm not a ghost. That's not really how this shit works. But if you come along for the ride, I promise I'll show you how it does.

First: Did you read the foreword? If you didn't, you're missing out. I don't want to be a dick about it, but my mom's got some really important stuff to say in there about who I was and what I was like when I was alive and why I'm even writing this memoir in the first place. So go back and read it now!

Second: As you can probably tell, I'm not what most people expect from a spirit guide from the afterlife. I still pretty much talk like I talked when I was alive. I swear, I sometimes forget what my point was and get frustrated with myself, and I never pull punches. Just thought you guys should know that up front. It's not my intention to be offensive or to turn people off. I want the opposite of that. Just a heads-up, though: I say what I mean and mean what I say, and sometimes how I say stuff isn't exactly poetry.

I'm here to share my story with you and to hopefully shed some light on what happens when we die and cross over into the spirit realm and all that cool shit. I hope you'll let me share these things with you. I guess that's what I want the most—to show people that life doesn't stop with death, not just tell them that it doesn't. It didn't for me. My "life" now is richer and more amazing and rewarding than it ever was when I was "alive," and it doesn't seem fair to keep that to myself. Helping people (including myself) wasn't something I could do when I was walking around on Earth, so I'm doing it now. I hope you'll be one of those people.

I

My Death

1

The End of Me

······································

I'd thought about suicide before.

In fact, I thought about it a lot in the couple of years leading up to when I decided to end my life. I even researched on the internet all the ways I could do it.

The year before I succeeded, I tried by taking an overdose of a medication called Provigil, but I wasn't successful. I think I must have died for a little bit then, though, because I saw my deceased aunt, Denise, who'd taken her own life, and my friend Ally, who'd died from an accidental gunshot wound just after our high school graduation. They were sitting on either side of me, holding my hands. Their presence gave me comfort. It also gave me the sense that I was in a different place, better than the one I was in at the time, and I remember it feeling so good. I knew I wanted to go back there.

The day after my first suicide attempt, Pappa and I were standing by his truck. He asked me why I wanted to die. After all, the sky was blue and beautiful that day and everything seemed calm. Nice. Happy. I told him that I just wished I wasn't here anymore. It was difficult to explain, and I know that that reason couldn't even begin to express how I was feeling or why I wanted to die, but it was as close as I could get. Eventually, I'd get my wish.

On the last day of my life, things started out like any other day for me—a ride on a roller coaster. Ever heard that expression "I'm on a roller coaster that only goes up?" Well, mine only went down. Or, more accurately, my ups never lasted long enough and my downs felt like they'd go on forever. When I woke up that morning, I remember thinking, "Damn, another day," but once I got out of bed, I felt this strange peace and calm. It was fleeting, though, because those familiar periods of inner darkness soon took over and sent me into a tailspin.

It wasn't like I'd planned, "This is going to be the day. This is going to be the moment." I didn't wake up that morning and say, "Today is the day I'm going to die." It was more of a combination of circumstances and triggers that led me to make the decision I made. That morning, my parents had found out that I'd pawned some of their stuff to buy this awesome hunting rifle. It even had a scope. I just wanted something exciting and new to make me feel better. They were so disappointed in me, and I was tired of making them feel like that all the time. To be clear, this wasn't the gun I used to end my life; this was just another object in a long line of new toys and experiences I chased after to try and fill the hole that my disease (bipolar disorder; I'll talk about that more later) was carving away in me.

I'd bought a pistol a couple of months before because I wanted to go to the range for target practice with my friend Valentin. During those months, I thought about the gun quite a bit. I knew it was there, hidden away in my room, and the thought of it was almost a comfort. It was right after my parents fussed at me that I made up my mind to kill myself again, but this time with the pistol. I knew that shooting myself would guarantee my death while the overdose of pills didn't. When my mom, my sisters, and my aunt Teri were about to leave for lunch—a lunch they would never have, as it turned out—I got up from the sofa in the living room and walked upstairs to go to my bedroom. They asked me if I wanted to go with them, but I told them no because I didn't want my sudden determination broken. I wanted to end the pain forever, and I was sure that this time I'd be successful. I felt a sense of resolution. Like surrender, but not in a bad way.

Once I was in my room, I started to pace. I think well when I walk. So I paced back and forth for a while and then sat at my desk, contemplating. Aunt Teri walked down the hallway from the guest room and stopped in front of my open door. She asked me if I wanted to come, but I told her I just wanted to chill for a while. I could feel her hesitation. I knew she wanted to convince me to change my mind, but I guess my blank stare was a sign that I wanted to be left alone. Then, Maria, our housekeeper came in to make my bed. I totally tuned her out, and I must have given her the impression that I wanted to be alone because she finished quickly and hurried out of the room. After she left, I started to think about the clothes I was wearing and how uncomfortable I felt in them. My clothes felt like a second layer of skin that I wanted to shed. I guess my actual skin felt that way too. Everything felt too close and too much.

Once Maria had left, that strange sense of peace I'd woken up with suddenly came over me again, and that peace expanded and expanded until I felt much larger than life. It was a really enticing feeling. I wanted to be consumed by it.

Along with that peaceful feeling, I remember my mind filling up with emptiness. I know what you're thinking. That sounds like a contradiction—"filling up with emptiness"—but that's how it felt. As I sat there, memories of the shitty-ass things that had happened in my life flashed before me, slicing through the calm: people being nice to me but then talking behind my back or times when I'd helped my friends and then realized that they'd never return the favor. I kept thinking things like, "That's fucked up," and "That's not fair." After a while, the emptiness took over completely.

I didn't think about how people would react to what I was going to do, and I didn't want to think about how upset my family would be with me. I didn't want to think about the hurt. I just wanted to get the result I was looking for: an escape.

I knew that if I really thought about it analytically, my consciousness would get a hold of me and pull me out of that inner peace I was desperate to hold on to. I wasn't interested in that. I was in such a calm place that when I thought about my mom and my dad, it was really about how much I loved them and how they were there for me and how much they supported me. I wasn't thinking, "They put me here," or "This is their fault," because they didn't and it wasn't. I wasn't thinking, "They didn't do anything to help," because they did. I was so far away from blaming anyone. That moment wasn't about any of that.

When I heard my mom, sisters, and aunt leave the house, I remember thinking, "This is it. Now is the right time." I kept the bullets in my closet and the gun in a drawer under my bed. I knew that if I kept the gun loaded and my parents found it, then I'd be without both, so I kept them separate. I loaded a bullet into the gun and sat down at my desk again. From that point on, I was on total autopilot. My mind was still blank, and it was almost like I had already separated from my body. Have you ever been driving in a car and then suddenly you're at your destination and you don't know how you got there? That was how it was for me. I was in a trance.

I usually fidget and wipe my hands on my legs when I'm about to do something I'm anxious about, but I wasn't even doing that. I was so relaxed. My hands weren't even sweaty. I felt no uneasiness. I knew what I was going to do. I had thought about it tons of times, and I knew how fast it was going to be. I had this image in my head that the gun would just blow away everything that was bad. It wouldn't blow away my family; it wouldn't blow away my connections. It would just blow away what I couldn't get control over. I didn't really see what I was doing as resulting in death, even though that sounds stupid, I know.

I saw it as an answer to blowing away that side of my brain that always seemed to work against me instead of for me.

I didn't think about where I'd end up after I died either. I just thought about darkness, and I knew I would be happy. I didn't doubt that at all, but I can't explain why. It wasn't like I thought that some god would come get me or that I'd fall into the arms of an angel or whatever, but it wasn't like I thought things would be over or that I'd disappear either. I thought that if there was something after death, good. If there wasn't, it'd be better than this. I saw it as a win-win situation. When I think about it now, I wish I would have given more thought to how my decision would affect the people in my life, but all I could think about right then was that all my pain would be gone if I just pulled the trigger and I would finally have relief.

My last thought before I did it was, "Okay." That's it. No good-byes. No thoughts or questions or worries. Just, "Okay." I placed the barrel firmly and without hesitation to the spot on my head that I knew would do the job. I felt peaceful.

Then, *bang.*

. . . .

I heard a ricochet sound, but I don't remember feeling anything other than the sensation that I was being jerked or pulled, but there was no burst of pain or sense of shock. Then, for a few seconds, there was nothingness.

Right after the gun went off, I heard Maria scream. She was vacuuming the den. Her scream kind of sounded like an ambulance siren. Maria's scream was probably the first sound I heard that connected what I had done to how it affected another person. It startled me and made me want to get up and go to her, but I stayed put in my room with my door closed. I remember the sound of her hurrying down the hallway. Then I heard her standing at my door for a few seconds. When she opened the door, she looked at me and screamed again—the kind of scream that would shatter glass.

I was standing in my room, but I had no idea how the fuck I was standing up because I had just shot myself in the head. I remember thinking, "Shit, I screwed it up. Maybe it didn't work!" I was confused. Disoriented. I looked down and saw my body, and that's when it hit me for real. "That's *me*," I thought. "That's my body." I won't lie; it did freak me out a little bit. I tried to get back into my body, but I couldn't, no matter how hard I tried. I remember thinking, "Okay, I can't get back in. I can't change things. This is the decision I made. Fuck, what have I done? I take it back! I see the value of life now. Just let me go back and I'll prove it!" Some part of me knew that I couldn't—that this was a done deal—but these sorts of thoughts bombarded me all the same. For a moment, I panicked, and I felt really disappointed in myself, especially because I realized then that everyone was going to find my body. I hadn't really processed how I was thinking these thoughts and feeling these emotions, since I was, you know, sitting there dead, but I know I thought and felt them all the same.

Next, my room sort of washed away like a fresh painting in the rain, and I felt like I was being pulled into the white of the canvas but still a part of the colors. At the same time, I wasn't separated from the room. It didn't feel like I went to an entirely different place. It wasn't like I was in the bedroom and went to the living room or in Houston and then went to London on a plane or something. I was in the fabric of everything. I didn't know what that meant yet, but I felt it.

As I looked around, it seemed like I had tunnel vision, and the periphery was all white. I didn't see my hand on the gun anymore. I didn't even see where the gun had gone after I'd shot myself. I didn't smell the gunpowder. That was weird, because I thought that if I were really in the room, wouldn't I have? I looked at my body through this narrow lens—this telescope—and although I knew it was me, I just couldn't connect to it emotionally. You know how when you see someone who's injured, it makes your stomach turn and your heart skips a beat and your adrenaline spikes, and it makes you want to run over to them to help? I didn't feel any of that.

My body looked like me, but it didn't *look* like me. I looked pale. My nose didn't look right. Even my fingers seemed too long. It was like I was looking at a cheap imitation of myself, a wax figure in one of those museums, a puppet without a puppeteer. Even though I didn't feel any empathy for my body, I had this need to put it back the way it had been only moments ago—sitting at my desk with a normal-looking head. I didn't want to, like, crawl back inside my body and reanimate it or anything; I just wanted to clean it up. I wanted to help.

The scene in front of me was so weird. It was like being in the movies and you see all that gory shit, and you say, "Oh, whatever. That's just entertainment." For me, it didn't seem like real life playing out right in front of me. It seemed separate from me, like it was playing on a screen, and I was in the audience watching, instead of being one of the actors.

I went to find the gun and pick it up. When I saw it and reached for it, I saw my new hand reaching for it. It didn't look light or translucent—you know, the type of thing that you would expect to see with a spirit or a ghost. It did have a kind of a glow to it, though. Silver, shimmery. I know it sounds weird, but it looked solid and transparent at the same time. Think about it: when you look at your reflection in dark water, it looks solid, but you know it's just a transparent reflection in the water. Meld those two, and that's what it looked like.

When I tried to grab or touch something, my hand went right through it. I guess it felt like a tingly pressure, but it didn't feel like regular touch. I tried to touch my body, but I couldn't grab ahold of it. Then I tried to strum the strings on my Fender guitar, but my fingers slipped through them too. No sound. I remember feeling pretty sad then, thinking that I'd never get to play music again.

Next, I heard my mother running up the stairs. I could tell she was climbing up the steps more than one at a time, tripping. She came into the room, but she didn't come in delicately. She came in like she was on fire—a flaming cannonball barreling through anything in its path. My point of view rose up like I was flying. I wasn't standing on the ground like a human. Even though I felt like I was hovering up high, I suddenly felt really small, like a child caught with his hand in the cookie jar. Still, I didn't feel the same kind of shame or sense of regret I expected to. I just felt small.

I don't want to sound like an asshole, but I didn't feel the need to rush to her. I had this emotional detachment while watching her, but it wasn't the same emotional distance I felt when I was about to pull the trigger or when I first left my body and looked down at it. It was an emotional distance that comes with an objective observation that made me feel separated from my feelings of remorse and shame.

When I left my body, my emotions came with me, but my physical instincts didn't, and that wasn't because of shock. Shock creates a distance you need for survival or protection when you have a physical body. I didn't need that anymore. Because of that emotional distance, my emotions weren't controlling me. Things were just playing out, and I was watching them while still feeling things, but in a different way. I believe I had that emotional distance so that I could continue to cross over with peace. I feel like I was in this weird dream state. Maybe that's what traumatic experiences turn into. They feel like a dream, no matter if you're a person or a spirit.

Despite that feeling of emotional distance, I was more aware—more sensitive but not more emotional, I guess. Because of this heightened awareness, I was able to absorb all the details of what was going on in the room. When you're human, you can't rely on your memory to look back accurately at traumatic situations because you can't consciously absorb all the details. Your brain picks and chooses some of the highlights, and you often leave out the ones that hurt the most. It was way different for me in those first few minutes after I died—and still is different today. It's just an objectivity that's intensely involved instead of highly removed. Being in that room with my mom, the emotional distance made it seem like what was going on was far away, but it didn't make it any less real.

My mom was talking to me, but she wasn't looking at the real me—my spirit. She was looking at my body. She kept wailing, "Why? Why? Why?" She had no problem touching my body, and she was the first person to move me, but I wasn't really in there at all. I was outside my body, watching her. There were two other people at the door peering at me—Maria and my sister Michelle. They weren't coming in, and nobody was inviting them to. I couldn't really focus on them; I was still fixated on what was happening to my physical body.

Even though I could see my mom crying over my body, I knew that everything was as it needed to be. It was weird, but I felt that to be true on a really deep level in those first few moments. It was a comfort to know that I didn't need to correct it or change what was happening, despite how hard it had to have been for those I left behind. I didn't yet know why it was going to be all right, but I just felt it would be.

I could see and hear everything and everyone in the house. Sounds seemed different than they did when I was in my body. They didn't sound as loud or clear. Everything sounded like it was underwater. I didn't have to travel anywhere to see things as they were happening. I wasn't interested in doing that anyway because I was so focused on watching this chapter of my life close. I was in awe as I objectively observed the end of "me"—something I never thought would happen. Ever.

Two policemen came into the room. One of the policemen was wearing something different. He wasn't in a police uniform. I guess he was a detective or something. Then there was another person who was with him, and I didn't understand what that dude's job was. I think it was to record—writing down and logging stuff. I didn't really know; I didn't really care. I went to the wall next to my bed and saw the hole in the wall where the bullet had ricocheted and ran my finger across it. I couldn't feel the dent, but I knew that it represented the hole I had just left in my mother's heart. I felt bad about that—really bad—but that didn't cancel out that strange feeling of everything being in its right place.

Eventually two paramedics came in. The detective gently led my mom out of the room. When she was gone, everyone stood around and talked—procedural things like what each one was supposed to do. They didn't react emotionally, really. You could tell they were trained to push aside their emotions and do their jobs without getting wrapped up in what they saw.

The first thing they did was discuss the time of death. One person was saying that they needed to get the story from Maria and my family. Then they came up with an estimated time of death. There were like four or five people in there going in and out of the room, up and down the stairs, doing their thing. They were wondering where the bullet was, whether it was still in my head or somewhere else, and eventually they found it. The policemen took pictures and measured things, like the gun, with a measuring tape. I heard a lot of rustling plastic. Everything went into plastic bags. Everything was sealed. Anything that was associated with my death was taken, but I cared less about these material things and more about what was happening to my body.

The two paramedics took my body out of the chair. One was on my left side; one was on my right side. When they picked me up, they didn't hold my head. Who would? So my head kind of flopped back. I guess that's the true definition of dead weight. Then they put me on the gurney. The body bag was already on top of it. They didn't undress me or anything. They tucked my feet into the bottom of the bag. The bag was more than big enough for me. I mean, it was *big*, and I remember the sound of the zipper. I just watched them zip me up. Then they talked about how they hated to leave the room the way it was and how my family would have to go in there and see all that. Later on, the crime scene cleanup crew came in with their masks on and cleaned up the mess, spraying luminol everywhere. It lit up all over the walls and even the ceiling. I could tell that they just looked at it as another job. One of them said they were glad a lot of time hadn't passed because it could have been a lot smellier. I realized that I could hear people's thoughts as I noticed that there was random shit going through everyone's mind. This didn't really shock me—nothing really shocked me as this was all happening, because of that pervasive feeling of rightness and detachment that surrounded me. I remember sensing that it wasn't a time for asking questions, even if there had been someone to answer them.

The moment I couldn't see my body, that's what made things more real. That body was no longer a part of me. Out of sight, out of mind. I didn't follow my physical body down the stairs and out the door; I was just suddenly outside. I knew they were taking me outside, and that's where I went. It was like blinking your eyes. One blink and you're in one place, and then another blink and you're in a different place. That was the first time I didn't travel like a human. I just appeared outside. I watched the doors of the ambulance close and wondered why they didn't just turn off the fucking lights, you know? No siren, though.

That's when I started to focus on what I was thinking, where I was, and what was happening with my spirit body. Transporting myself with my thoughts like that was an ability that felt very new to me as a free spirit, and I remember just sort of taking it in stride and going, "Huh. Cool." I was really curious, but I also knew that I had some stuff to take care of before I moved on to wherever I was going to go.

I didn't follow my body to the morgue or watch them do the autopsy. It wasn't necessary. As soon as my physical body got zipped up, that's when I truly started to realize that I wasn't just going to fade away into the air or whatever. I was, in some way, sticking around. At that point, I knew it was time to say my good-byes. I'd just said good-bye to me. Well, I really didn't say good-bye; I just watched my body get zipped up. But it was gone. I was over for me. Once that had happened, I really started to think about everyone else.

2

My Good-byes

···

I knew that I needed to say good-bye to my family and friends. Technically speaking, my good-byes weren't really good-byes. I just wanted my family members and friends to know that I was okay, that I still existed somehow, and that I appreciated all they'd given to me. I felt like I had done them wrong in the sense that I didn't give them a chance to say good-bye to me. I was ready, but they weren't. That's where I'd kind of fucked up. Looking back now, I realize that I was already helping people when I was saying my good-byes.

Connecting to the people I love became easy after I died. The emotional distance I had at the beginning that I found so damn useful disappeared with that body bag after it was zipped up. I didn't need that distance anymore. In a way, it was great because now (you know how we talk about using our five senses to emotionally and physically connect) as a spirit, I not only had those five senses but I also had this whole other palette of emotions that I could use to reach out and connect. I could sense people's feelings and hear their thoughts. I realized this new power was coming from me and that it was a natural sense, just like sight or hearing or smell but unique to my new plane of existence, whatever that was. It was part of me, and it made me feel bigger and better and happier. Because I could tap into each one of my family members' and friends' feelings and thoughts, I decided to tailor every good-bye to how each person would have liked to experience it and what would be best for them. They couldn't see or hear me, but I hoped that somehow it would soak in. And it turned out that it did.

It wasn't like I was stuck with just picking up the phone and going, "Hey, man. I love you. Take care. Bye," or like I stood in front of them with a bullhorn and shouted. I just sat next to them and talked, and since they processed everything I said energetically, I could give them the sensation or gut feeling that everything was going to be okay. I told each of them that I loved them, that I was leaving, and that I was going to be fine.

When I think back on who I said my good-byes to and when, I realized that memories from every relationship were different for me. It's not like when I was human and could think back into the past. It seemed like everything was stuck in the present and that there was no past or future—like I was experiencing my entire relationship with each person simultaneously, but it wasn't overwhelming or scary; it just felt right. Later, I would learn that where I am, time is not linear like it is on Earth, so that means that memory and timelines and shit work differently for me than they do for you, but if I try to line it up in Earth time, here's basically how it went:

I said bye to my sisters and brother first. I started with Kristina. I visited her at her house the night of my death. She was lying on her couch with the covers pulled up around her chin, trying to digest the events of that day. I could see that she was both shaken and in shock from processing everything that had just happened. At the same time, she was numb. Can you be numb and shocked at the same time? I didn't really know, but that's how it seemed to me.

Kristina wasn't angry with me right after my death, though. That would come later. It was fucking horrible to sense that from her when it did. She felt some remorse, too, because right before my death, I'd texted her to tell her that Mom had given me her old iPhone and I was so proud and excited, but she felt a little annoyed with me and didn't text me back. That would have been the last time I talked to her.

Because she was the oldest, I always thought of Kristina as "Miss Fix It," but not in a bad way. She cares for everybody like it's her responsibility, but she loves doing it. She didn't want to believe that my death was real because I think she felt that if she did, it meant that it somehow would have been her job to save me, even though that would have been impossible. I don't think she wanted to believe that I'd died by taking my life either.

Her grief was absent and disconnected so she could protect herself from it. That absence was like a wall all around her, so it made it hard for me to get close to her. I also realized that if I did, it would make things too real for her, and she would shut down. I had to use the happy memories of the things we'd done together so she wouldn't just concentrate on what had just happened and get overwhelmed.

Once I was able to reach Kristina through those memories, I sat beside her and told her all the things she'd taught me. That's what I did with everyone I said good-bye to. I told them what I'd learned from them. With all my sisters and my brother, I learned that whenever they got on my nerves or when I didn't feel like they were in my corner that it wasn't about me; it was about their own shit. I think that's how it works with pretty much everybody, you know? Anyway, with Kristina, I told her that she taught me how you have to protect your heart. You can't always walk around with it fully exposed like I had. Some people who protect their hearts are misunderstood. They're seen as cool or aloof, but they can still feel deeply, and Kristina does.

After Kristina, I said good-bye to my sister Michelle. I remember that right after my death, she was pacing in front of my mom, who was sitting on the couch in our living room. Then Michelle announced that I was in a better place and walked off. I guess that came from her denial. Later that night, I went to her apartment and sat down next to her on her bed. I could tell she was wondering why she couldn't have fixed me and why she couldn't solve the problem that had unfolded in front of her. She wanted to turn back the clock and erase all the times we'd fought and all the times she'd shut me out.

I nicknamed Michelle "the grave digger" because she kind of had to dig me up in her mind after I was dead to fully process that I was gone. Besides Maria and my mom, she was the only one who saw me after I'd shot myself, so she had to see that graphic image again in her mind and talk about it out loud to know that it was real. That was the only way she could wrap her head around what had happened. Maybe she thought that would give her closure.

Michelle was in so much shock that I had to pretty much sit on top of her and hold her down to help her control her thoughts about me and eventually be okay with saying good-bye. While I was with her, I noticed she was thinking about dozens of thoughts at once, most of them in the form of "why?" Why hadn't she seen it coming? Why hadn't she been more aware? There were also lots of hows, whats, and whens floating around in her head: How did I come to the decision to leave? How was she going to be able to move forward? How was she going to talk about it with other people, like what was appropriate to talk about and what wasn't? Michelle also wanted to know when I'd started thinking about it and when I'd come to the conclusion to take my own life. What made it especially hard for her was that we had had a falling out a few weeks before, so fleeting moments of guilt and regret washed over her while I sat with her. Then when each of those moments passed, she eventually realized that it wasn't about her, and I think that that helped her a lot.

While I sat with Michelle, I learned a ton from her. We had been very close and had spent a lot of time together, so I told her that she'd taught me what it's like to be a real friend, but I also learned that, with friendships, you can sometimes tear each other apart, and that can be the path to sewing yourself together into a new and better you.

Next came Lukas. I hung around him in the backyard for a while and then followed him back into the house. I walked by his side and followed him up to his bedroom. When he sat down on his bed, I sat next to him. Other than my mom, he was more in shock than anyone else. It was so overwhelming for him that he couldn't even get a sense of how his body felt.

I could sense that the energy of every cell in Lukas's body was quivering and vibrating at a higher-than-normal rate. He couldn't believe I was dead. Lukas thinks very analytically, and he couldn't find the logic behind what I'd done, so the whole thing didn't make sense to him. One of his thoughts was, "If Erik can do this, then anyone can." This made him question the concept of the value of life.

I tried to calm his body down so that his cells wouldn't vibrate at such a high frequency and so that he could feel okay again. He was numb. He couldn't feel his emotions; I guess that's because he's the kind of guy who feels later, after he's had a chance to process things. Lukas is the one in the family who wants to feel but tucks everything away instead of fully immersing himself in his emotions. I should have done more of that. I kind of fucked things up for him because my death caused him to stuff his emotions down even more, and that makes me feel like a dick, but I did learn something from the way he handled his feelings, both after my passing and in general: I learned that it's okay to take your time. Instead of jumping right into the pool, you can walk around the edge and figure out which side you want to jump from. Then you can stick your toe in to test the water. You have to jump into your pool of feelings eventually. With Lukas, he's about observing things and taking his time before making a decision about something or deciding what to feel. I thanked him for teaching me that.

Then came my sister Annika. A couple of hours after I died, she went upstairs to her bedroom, and I sat beside her. I could see that she was trembling and crying. Her energy looked like shattered glass that had been glued back together. Right then, she had no way of mending or counseling herself, so she felt extremely helpless and useless.

I sensed the weight on Annika's shoulders. She tends to feel responsible for everyone else, and now she felt a responsibility for helping my mom get through the day. Annika didn't know how she could help her. She didn't even know if she could, but she knew she had to try, so in spite of her grief, she sacrificed the opportunity to heal herself and immediately concentrated on helping my mom. She wanted to make sure Mom was okay. In fact, right after I died, she got a wet paper towel and gently wiped the blood off of my mom's hands—the blood that had come from hugging my body. Annika wanted to do something. Anything.

Annika was also pissed. She couldn't understand why this was happening. She couldn't believe that I had put her in this situation. She couldn't believe that I had put *anyone* she loved in this situation.

As I sat with her, I told her that she needed to take care of herself first. Otherwise, she wouldn't be in any kind of shape to help anyone else. Taking care of herself meant that she had to love herself enough to put her own needs before anyone else's. That's how it works for everyone, not just her. I also told Annika that I wish I had taken better care of her, my baby sister. She was always wiser and more collected than I ever had been. That made her seem like she didn't need anything from anyone, including me, but now I see that she was just putting on a brave front. She tries to be strong for everyone in the family, but she's more fragile inside than she lets on. I guess that's why I'd never reached out to her. I'd had troubles of my own, so that made helping my family members difficult. It kind of made me a selfish asshole sometimes. Depression can do that to a person.

From Annika, I learned that you can't carry everyone's burdens like I'd done. Not only had I carried other people's burdens sometimes but I also had carried my own burdens alone. I could have reached out to somebody so that they could help me carry my load.

I thanked Annika for teaching me that, and I hope she continues to learn to lean on the people she loves when she needs to.

Next came Aunt Teri. Poor Aunt Teri. She lives in California and doesn't know her way around the city, and she was the one who drove my mom and Michelle home when Maria called them to let them know she'd heard something that sounded like a gunshot from my room. Then when Maria screamed into the phone after seeing me dead, things got crazy. I don't know how she kept it together enough to get home. She almost seemed like she was out of her body. All that day and for a few days after my death, Aunt Teri handled pretty much everything. She was the one who was in control. She arranged for the cleanup crew to come over; she helped us choose songs for the funeral; and she even helped figure out what to write on my grave marker. Aunt Teri's used to being in control of everything. She's usually pretty fucking good at it, too, but this was one time things didn't go according to her plans. Don't worry. I'm getting to the point soon. This is just the backstory.

So, on the day I died, after the cleanup crew left, Aunt Teri lay down on one of the couches in the den and went to sleep. While she was dreaming, I felt her sorrow. She felt so bad that she hadn't been able to convince me to go out for lunch with everyone. She thought that maybe if she had insisted, then I would have gone with them— and then I wouldn't be dead. How could she live with that? I told her that I was okay and that I was free. That was my good-bye to her.

With Aunt Teri, my good-bye was about cutting her loose. That's how she understands a good-bye. You take a person to the airport, drive them to the passenger drop-off lane, give them a hug, and say, "Have a nice trip." Then you drive home. One thing I learned from Aunt Teri is that sometimes you have to run away in order to find yourself. She'd done that when she was young. She'd left home to escape her abusive parents, and by doing so, she had been able to build a life for herself and get to know the person she was with the pain peeled away. So she taught me that running away isn't always a bad thing. You sometimes have to leave the situation to understand who you are, and that takes courage.

Then I said good-bye to Uncle Jim. I love Jimbo. Uncle Jim tried to teach me how to fish, but that didn't work out too well because I was too fucking impatient. I wanted to catch a fifteen-pound bass a few seconds after tossing my line in the water, but to be honest, I think I'd only caught one fish in my life, and it probably weighed under a pound. Looking back, I'm glad he tried to teach me all the same, though.

I didn't visit Jim until a couple of days later. He was at his apartment, sitting outside on the back porch, smoking. He looked detached, disconnected from everything. I knew he was too far removed from the world to feel my presence, but I sat in the chair next to him anyway. Even though he was shut off from everything, Uncle Jim was still consumed with sorrow, which is weird for him because he's not a big feeler. He was so confused. He kept thinking over and over again, "Was this really the news? Is this all real?" Things didn't really sink in for him until much later. That's just how grief works sometimes.

I thanked Uncle Jim for all the things he'd taught me. He never puts his foot in his mouth, so that taught me that it's sometimes necessary to bite your tongue. He has a lot of integrity and a strong work ethic, and that taught me that there are things you have to do in life because it's the right thing to do, even if you don't really want to. Sometimes you have to do some really fucked-up shit. Sometimes it's just boring or it's a grind or it's uncomfortable, but you have to do it and get through it all the same.

When I was with Uncle Jim, I said good-bye to Aunt Laura too. She was pacing nervously in front of him, chain-smoking. She liked her cigs. I wanted to comfort her, so every once in a while I'd get up from my chair and walk alongside her. She was out of control, full of panic and shock at the same time. I thought she was about to explode. She was also scared because she thought that if this had happened to me, who'd be next? She's pretty morbid and thinks about death a lot anyway.

Aunt Laura was my friend, my confidante, my smoking buddy. Sometimes she'd sneak me a cigarette now and then, warning me not to say a word to my mom and dad. Both of us didn't want to get busted.

In Aunt Laura, I saw myself: misunderstood. Once I was out of my body, I learned things about her that I didn't know when I was alive. I could see all the struggles she had gone through, and I commiserated with her because my life had sucked too. But then I thought, "If she got through them—and her struggles were darker, tougher—then why couldn't I get through *mine*?" I didn't yet understand that my struggles on Earth were part of my larger purpose, but from Aunt Laura, I still learned what strength is. I thanked her for that and said good-bye.

After Aunt Laura came Maria. Maria didn't like that she had been the first one to find me and that she had been involved in some way in my exit. I definitely can't blame her for that; it couldn't have been easy. She'd taken care of me since I was eighteen months old, so she was like a second mother. I visited her early on the morning after my death. She was back at her house on her knees, praying. I could see her whole body shaking. Tears were running down her cheeks. She was so sad. Just so sad. It was the type of sadness that made me want to cry with her. I wanted to comfort her, so I kneeled next to her and held her hand. Even though she was trembling and crying, I could feel that she was still a force to be reckoned with. I felt this peace and strength inside her that I hadn't recognized before.

While I was with her, she talked out loud to me. She says these out-loud prayers sometimes, and she was in the middle of one of those when I came to her. I think her prayers were how she handled her grief. It's like we had a conversation, in a way. First she told me that things would be okay. She had this sense of knowing that I would be fine. She also thought about what she could have done if she had gotten there faster and if she had reacted differently. She wished that she had noticed something when she was in my room making up my bed, even though I think we both knew that there really was nothing she could have said or done in those moments to change the situation.

I told Maria how grateful I was that she'd taught me about playfulness and about letting go, even when you don't feel like it. I also told her how much I appreciated how she would patiently let me talk to her about things she wasn't interested in. Her English was not very good when I was growing up, so sometimes she would pretend like she was listening. It meant so much to me that even when she didn't understand everything I was saying and even though she was busy with her responsibilities in the house, she would take the time and stay with me, like that time I tried to give her directions on how to re-spoke a bicycle wheel. From Maria, I learned that sometimes you have to make sacrifices for the people you care about. I learned that you have to be patient, like her.

I visited a few of my friends the day after my death too. Valentin was in his house, sitting on his bed, talking to himself with his head in his hands. I sat next to him and put my arms around him. Friends are not supposed to make each other feel that fucking way.

Valentin was the one I had spent the most time with the last few months I was alive. He had made those months so great. Valentin could relate to me because he sometimes felt like an outsider too. I wanted him to know that my death was a happy moment, so I made him pick up on the playful personality I'd had when I was around him during the good times we shared. That way, he could feel that it was really me beside him. This made him laugh at inappropriate times about stuff: that I was able to get the hell out of my life before the shit hit the fan, struggling, getting old, things like that. I guess he was thinking, "You lucky bastard" while he was chuckling inside.

See, Valentin had bought the gun I'd used for me because he was twenty-one and I wasn't. The only reason he'd bought it was because I'd wanted to go to target practice with him. Still, *he* didn't pull the trigger. I did. So he shouldn't feel guilty or responsible. I hope he knows that.

As I sat with him, I thanked him for teaching me what trust is, that there are people you can trust and that there are friends that will be able to handle things when they get heavy. Valentin was that person for me.

Then I visited my parents. Pappa came first. Oh, Pappa. There he was, standing in front of the desk in the kitchen. As I stood by his side, I could see that he was closed down, zipped up. His face was flushed, and his feet were tingling. He didn't want to believe it was real. It was like he was watching a horror movie unfolding in front of him. The thing is, a lot of horror movies end up with the bad guy or the swamp monster or whatever getting killed and everyone that was in danger being saved, so the movie ends on a happy note. That wasn't the way it was that day, and Pappa didn't understand why he couldn't rewrite the ending.

His energy felt elastic, but I still couldn't get past his barriers to access it. It was like trying to get into a tent without unzipping the flap first. He was different because I'd been able to merge my energy with everybody else's during my good-byes. I had to wait until he was angry because when he was, he could open up that tent. You have to get big when you're angry. Anger is actually a really vulnerable emotion that opens you up a little bit. Part of his anger was because he felt helpless and useless. Pappa's used to controlling everything and protecting everyone he loves. Because he couldn't control whether his son would live or die, he sort of crumbled and became a little boy again.

I always wanted to have a connection with Pappa, but he didn't let me into his world as much as I wanted him to. After I died, I still had that human pain of not having the connection I wanted, but I didn't need his approval anymore. I didn't need his attention. Instead, I got his attention by loving him. It was an "I forgive you" love. It was an "everything is okay between us" love. I really couldn't give him that when I was alive. I always felt Pappa wasn't open to that kind of thing anyway. He's Norwegian, so I guess it's a cultural thing too. Scandinavians don't usually get all emotional and gooey like people in some other countries do. Not that that's bad or anything. It's just how they are.

I realized two things then about Pappa that I hadn't realized before. I used to think he was trying to teach me lessons to keep me in line and that's what made the distance between us, but he just wanted to protect me, and the only way he knew how to do that was by talking "at" me instead of "with" me. He didn't know how to get involved. He thought I was supposed to know things or behave a certain way even though nobody had taught me or shown me how, so when I didn't act or think the way he thought I should, he'd fuss at me. It was his way of trying to protect me from myself.

Even though I first came to him when he was standing in the kitchen that day, it wasn't until the day after I died that I decided to say good-bye to Pappa. I came to him in a dream. In the dream, he was standing by his kickass Ford F-450 Super Duty. I loved that fucking truck. I stood behind him and told him I was okay. He asked me why I had wanted to leave, and I leaned to the right, into his energy, and said, "This is how I felt before." Immersed in my energy, he was overcome by all the emotions I felt when I was alive: the despair, the confusion, the sadness, and the hopelessness. I had to pull away from him to get him out of that horrible black cloud. Then I leaned to the left, back into his energy, and said, "This is how I feel now." When I did that, he felt my happiness, my relief, and my sense of freedom. That was my way of telling him that I'm okay—that I'm actually better than okay.

From Pappa, I learned why he didn't always want me to do certain things with him, like riding motorcycles. When I was alive, I thought he just didn't want to be around me. Now I know that he was teaching me that you can't always do whatever the hell you want. Sometimes you have to have someone there to pull you back. Pappa understood that in order to learn boundaries and safety, you have to do things at a slower pace. You can't just jump out of a plane without a parachute. Even though I wanted to have a shared hobby with him, like racing motorcycles, I couldn't jump on the bike and race around the track with what little experience I had. It was a good thing, too, because I'm clumsy and easily distracted, like my mom.

Of everyone in my immediate family, I visited my mom last because I had to work up the courage for it. Visiting everyone else in the family first gave me more strength to be in the presence of her grief. I was timid saying good-bye to her in particular because her emotions were so overwhelming. She wasn't even in her body. She was just a lost shell of herself. That made her completely numb, so I don't think she could have had any feelings just then.

While the cleanup crew was finishing up upstairs, she was in her bedroom, lying on her side. I sat next to her for a while. When I finally mustered up the courage to say good-bye—when I went to embrace her and to show her that I was around and that I was okay— she was too far removed to hear my words or feel my presence. She was deep inside her head, trying to understand what the fuck had just happened. See, my mom's a doctor. Her main calling in life is to help fix, heal, and cure, and for her, it's like putting the pieces of a puzzle together. She sees her patients as a big puzzle with a lot of pieces, so she doesn't just try to figure out what's wrong with them; she wants to know about all other the other pieces of their puzzle, like if there was anything in their personal life that might affect their health: their relationships, their family life, their emotional health, their financial troubles, and things like that. As a doctor, that makes her pretty unique. She's like the unicorn of doctors.

Once she understands the whole puzzle, my mom tries to make her patients well by helping them put all their broken pieces together in the right place. She wanted to do the same thing with me, but she wasn't seeing all my shattered pieces for what they were in those moments after my death; she was just focused on wanting to put me back together again, even though that wasn't possible. She wanted to put the puzzle of my death together, not take it apart. She thought that putting the pieces together would help her, kind of like sewing the arms, the legs, the eyes, and the mouth back onto a torn-up doll.

What she really needed to do was take the puzzle apart and get to know each piece instead of immediately try to patch things back together. That's the only way she'd be able to better understand my death and everything surrounding it. She needed to see that piece that represented the "why," the piece that represented the fact that my death was my choice, not something she could have prevented, the piece that represented the state of mind I needed to be in in order for me to pull the trigger, and the piece that represented her acceptance that death is a transition, not a permanent separation. That's how she would eventually start the healing process, but she wasn't there yet. If she had been in that space, it would have been easier for me to get through to her, but it was too early. Every time I tried to get close to her and say my good-bye, it triggered the terror all over again. Terror mixed with numbness. Not a pretty thing. That's why I couldn't sit down next to her for very long when she was lying in her bedroom that day.

When you're human and you're in tune with what's going on—call it "centered" or whatever—it's like you have one pipe that your emotions are flowing through, nice and simple. After my death, it was as if my mom sprouted a dozen leaks in that pipe, and I couldn't connect to the pipe and stop up those leaks. My mom was trying to use all these crazy emotions spilling around in her to understand my death, but she didn't even know where she was going or where she was coming from in order to begin. At the same time, she was trying to deal with the immense grief and pain of being the mom who couldn't save her own child.

Once I was dead, I got to see all of the struggles she had gone through from childhood on. I even got to see what struggles she was going to have in the future. Seeing that made me want to figure out how to make her whole again. I knew that I had to wait until she woke up and reached out for answers. I had to wait until she was ready to talk about her experience, and I had to wait until she was ready to see that I'm still living and I'm okay.

I tried to get her to feel that when I was in her room with her, but she wasn't feeling anything. That's not to say she didn't have any emotions, because I already described the ones she was dealing with at that moment, but she was too numb to feel them in a way that made sense to her. See my dilemma? I fucking wanted to wake her up, but I couldn't touch her. I wanted to tell her I was okay, but she couldn't hear me. It was beyond frustrating. Times like those are when it really sucks being a spirit. I knew that it sucked even before I really knew I was a spirit.

From my mom, I understood what a soul mate is. I could literally see the core connection we had. It was unbreakable. Still is. From her, I learned that bonds like ours can't be broken. That's love. Everyone else I said good-bye to represented a different flavor of love, and she was one of those flavors too. She was my favorite flavor.

After I finished my good-byes to my family in Houston, I thought about my mom's father, Poppi, because he was the one who didn't believe in any of this life-after-death shit I was experiencing, and he's old. He should have died a long time ago, and I didn't want him to die thinking there was nothing after death. Nobody else was going to bring it up to him, so why not put it right into his fucking lap?

I wanted to show him that there is a life or a consciousness or whatever you want to call it after you die, even though I was still a very young spirit and didn't fully understand how all that shit worked yet. So I showed up at his house. I simply thought about him, and there I was. He was in a chair in his living room. I stood in front of him, and he didn't see me. I stood there longer, and he still didn't see me. So I turned myself into the age when he remembered me best—when I was little. He saw me then. He reacted first with horror, fear, and confusion. I could feel those emotions rolling off of him in waves. He was thinking, "Have I lost my mind? This can't be real. Am I dying? Am I dying?"

I knew he couldn't explain it, and I wanted him to really, really know it was real. I wanted Poppi to *feel* it. I suddenly knew I had to crawl into his lap like I used to do when I was a kid. So I did, and I looked into his eyes. I told him that everything was fine and that I loved him. Then I told him good-bye. I touched his face, and he watched me. He didn't talk back to me. He made some sounds, though. It was funny to see his reaction, and that fed me even more light, more energy, because I cracked open his mind a little bit. He didn't hug me or anything, but just from seeing his shock, it felt like I had done the right thing. It felt so good. In retrospect, I see that I was helping him face his fears, and I planted that seed in his mind that things don't end at death.

Later, he called my mom and told her about the whole experience. She knew Poppi was stubborn as shit when it came to his beliefs, so that caused the first spark of hope in her that maybe I wasn't gone for good. I mean, fuck, the first words he said to her after she came crying to his house were, "Sorry, Elisa, but Erik is going to turn to dust." He had a point (that is pretty much what happened to my physical body, after all), but who says that to a grieving mother, man? Anyway, that big, knotted mass of skepticism and doubt started to unwind like a ball of yarn inside both Poppi and Mom for the very first time.

Last, I went to see Pappa's father, Bestefar. I sat next to him and put my hand on his leg. He gave me the feeling that he felt me. It's like when you have that sense that you're being watched but you can't put your finger on why. In him, I felt a sadness that was there even before I died and even before my grandmother Bestemor died. He's carried that sadness around for a long time. From him, I learned that it's important to let go of certain things. Sometimes he didn't do that. He's lost a lot of people in his life, and he's afraid that if he lets go of the grief, he'll lose the memory of that person. I tried to hug him and comfort him. I told him that everything was going to be okay. I really wanted him to know how much I loved and appreciated him because I didn't get to say that much to him before.

I guess I just wanted both of my grandfathers to know that there's more to the death process than just that—dying. Neither of them believed that there is something greater after death, and it isn't just something sad and to be dreaded. I also knew that I was going to see them on the other side before I saw the rest of my family.

Looking back, I realize I was already helping people when I was saying my good-byes. That was the beginning of my role as a guide, and that's sweet. With each person I visited, I just got happier and happier. When I was finished—I don't really know how to say this—I started to *get* who I was for the first time since that moment in my room with the gun. I started to feel complete. I could look at my relationships with everyone without my brain or body getting in the way, and that pure knowing touched me on a level I didn't even know I had.

3

My Funeral

....

I hung around my family for the days leading up to my funeral. I was still getting used to being whatever I was—I still wasn't really all that focused on who or what I had become then, since it was all so new. I didn't feel very tethered to my experiences. I wanted to make sure I wasn't dreaming, so I kept asking myself if everything that was happening was real. It was almost like I was fact-checking. "Is this real? Check. Are you sure it's real? Check. Are you *absolutely positive*? Yeah, man, I'm sure!" I definitely didn't understand everything yet, but there was no denying that it was actually happening.

Everyone was really bummed out during the days right after my death, of course. There were bits of lightness and humor, though. I remember that. Like the day before the funeral, my uncle and aunt from Norway were sitting around the breakfast table listening to my dad, and whatever he said made them burst into laughter. Sometimes the best medicine for grief is laughter.

Two days after I died, my mom and dad had to go to the funeral home to make the arrangements. My mom walked around like a zombie, looking at one plot selection to the next. Then they picked out a casket, and I was there in the casket room with them. They chose a really pretty one that had music notes on the corners. That was nice because they knew how much I loved my music. Still, it felt super weird that they considered the casket my final home. My body wasn't me—*I* knew that, but they didn't. At least not yet.

It was hard to listen to my mom and dad discuss what clothes I should be buried in. At first they said it'd be nice for me to be dressed in jeans, but then they decided to dress me in one of my suits. I loved wearing suits. They made me feel really important, and I hadn't felt like that in life very much. Sometimes I'd just dress up in my suit for no reason and walk around the house, strutting like a proud rooster. I called them my "Pappa suits" because my dad wore them to work every day.

On the day of the funeral, I could see everyone getting ready. I sensed the heaviness in everyone's energy. It's hard to describe. It was like a thick fog, and that fog had my name written all over it. My mom in particular seemed really detached. A part of her just went away that day, I think. I didn't feel any negative emotions toward me coming from her, but I still wanted to hang my head down with sadness.

Then I went to the funeral home. I wasn't required to go. No one made me. It was like there was this pull, like a kid sitting in front of a bowl of ice cream, and even though he's told he can't have it, he can't stop himself.

First, I hung around where my body was. There were family members around me that I knew were already dead. It wasn't so much that I could see them but more like I could sense them. I felt like they were there to support me and let me know that I wasn't alone. I knew they had my back.

I looked at my body in the open casket and thought how much it didn't look like me. I still couldn't identify with it, so it didn't really bother me. It was pretty surreal. When you die, it's not like you're all,

"Run, bitch, run! Don't look toward the light!" You don't have that kind of fear or anxiety, and you get to a place where you know you can't go back anyway, so you feel this objective, detached resignation—definitely a sense of peace. Another thing is that you see your body as a shell. It's like you're a snake that's just shed its skin, so when you look at yourself, it really doesn't look like the person you were before. How can you get all emotional about that? So there's nothing to handle emotionally because you don't have any emotions about it to begin with. It's the emotional ramifications your passing has on other people that gets you emotional.

While I was looking at my body, I started talking to myself, saying things like, "Boy, did you fuck up." In that moment, I really wasn't very understanding of the struggles I had gone through when I was alive. I was starting to feel like I'd made a mistake. But at the same time, I felt that my body lying there in the casket represented the closure of a chapter of some sort and that it was right that that chapter was over. I did feel some sense of completion when my body was being zipped up in the body bag, but this was different. It was like when I'd have to do a book report in school. I was the type of person who'd worry about it right up until it was due, and I'd fret over how much work it would take instead of actually doing the work. Then when it was done and I'd turned it in, I'd feel relieved. That's the type of completion I'm talking about. A sense of relief, even if things weren't perfect. When I was there beside my casket, I was thinking about all the things I could have—and maybe should have—done differently. But it was no use because the book report had already been turned in. This was how things had turned out.

Next, I was at the service. Just like I had instantly traveled outside from my bedroom the day I died as soon as I thought about going outside, I was suddenly at the service. It didn't weird me out, this new way that time and space were working. Like I said earlier, I wasn't really focused on the concept of "me" so much as what was going on around me in those first few days.

Oh yeah, my service. It was kind of surreal—no, it *was* surreal—witnessing my own funeral. I hovered around the cars of the people showing up. A lot of my friends came, even the ones who weren't so nice to me. I realized as I watched them that what they had done to me had nothing to do with me; it had to do with their own shit, like peer pressure or things that were happening in their own families. It was like I suddenly understood the plotline of their movies. I felt compassion for them instead of getting upset or disappointed, and that's when I realized that I couldn't hold on to negative emotions like I could before I died, even if I tried to. I might feel them for a split second, but they quickly evaporated. They were like drops of water falling into a hot skillet and completely sizzling away.

I remember everybody filing through the door and sitting in their seats. I followed my family in at the same time I hovered around my open casket. That was the first time I realized that I could split off and be in multiple places at the same time, and it happened naturally, like breathing when I was alive. I watched my mom. She seemed like she was in another world. She had moments when she'd tear up, but then she'd pull herself together and meet people with a smile, kind of like being a host at a dinner party. Everybody deals with grief differently, and my mom deals with it by focusing on the comfort of other people.

At some point, I realized that I could hear what sounded like a thousand voices in the room. Some of them were talking to me but not in the way that they would if we were having a direct conversation. It was more like they were talking *to* me, not *with* me. Some people asked me why I'd done it. Some told me they loved me and missed me. Some asked me if I was all right. Whether they were talking to me or about me, it came right to me in a big symphony of voices.

The weird thing is that if there were twenty people talking about me, those twenty conversations came right to me all at once, even if they were talking about me to somebody else. Not only did I hear everyone's inner thoughts but I also *felt* their emotions. It wasn't confusing, just overwhelming. If I were able to slow down and think about it logically, I would have thought that I should have been totally confused, because who can handle so many conversations at once or feel that many things at once? I'm not talking about what feelings they were projecting to people around them. I'm talking about what they *really* felt inside. If I were to freak out about the whole being-dead thing, that would have been the time I'd have done it. I didn't, though. I just let it wash over me and through me. It was intense, but it also felt right.

The best part about my funeral was that I felt so much love around me. There was so much laughter. It wasn't what I would have expected a funeral to be like. Sure, I felt sadness, but I felt happiness too. People shared their stories of what they remembered about me, what I had done for them and how much they appreciated it. I didn't get to hear those things when I was alive. It made me wonder why people don't share that shit more often in life, you know? No one should wait for death to share how they really feel.

The place was packed, and I was above everybody. It was weird because it wasn't like I was above people, looking at the top of their heads or their hair. Even though I was above everything, when I thought about someone, I could instantly see their face without being in front of them. Let's say I was thinking about my sister Annika when I was alive but we weren't in the same room. I would be able to see her face in my mind. It was kind of like that, but unlike before I died, where I could imagine Annika's face based on a memory I had of her, now I could be behind her and still be able to see her face right then and there—not the memory of her face but her real face in the present. That was freaky. I wasn't really comfortable with it, but I didn't know how to stop it either, so I just flowed with it because what choice did I have?

I moved around the room a lot. I never could stay in one place when I was alive, and it was no different during the service. Sometimes I'd be in the center and then in front, and sometimes I'd sit by my family to give them what comfort I could.

My funeral was the first time since my death that I was confronted by everyone's descriptions of me—like who I was to them. I was also confronted with their disbelief that I'd taken my own life. Not many people, other than my family, understood that at all, because they didn't know the pain I had suffered throughout my life. Most of my family didn't need to ask why. They already knew, but there were a hell of a lot of "whys" floating around from other people in the audience:

Why didn't he just ask for help?

Why did he do it at home?

Why didn't he see that what he did was inconsiderate?

Why didn't he think about the horror his parents would feel when they found him?

I wanted to sit down and tell my story to everybody, but at the same time, I didn't feel like it was necessary. I didn't feel like I had to explain my perspective or correct their opinions. It's almost like I was Scrooge in *A Christmas Carol* having to observe what was happening without interfering with or changing things.

Then came the eulogies. That's when the people in the audience became fixated on the speaker, so there were fewer voices coming at me. That part of the service was amazing because it was the time it felt like everyone was in unison. Everybody was connecting to the same thought. Everybody was coming together. There's not a word that can describe how the energy in the room made me feel. It was more overwhelmingly healing than anything I'd ever experienced. When somebody stood up and spoke to the crowd and everyone was listening to what that person had to say, I understood how special and loved I was—something I couldn't see when I was alive. I'd never felt special, even though my family tried to make me see that I was. I just didn't know how to receive that. I was blocked from this knowledge, but the words in the eulogies destroyed that blockage and I was finally able to connect to the love I couldn't connect to in life. I'm so grateful for that.

When my mom gave her eulogy, I felt like I needed to hold her up. I felt like I needed to help her finish it. It was the first time that I felt deeply sorry for more than a fleeting moment.

I don't remember traveling with the casket when the pallbearers were carrying it out. Instantly, I was at the graveside service. Honestly, the service totally kicked ass because there was just enough religion and just enough "real talk" to make people say good-bye without thinking they'd missed something. There was something for everyone, the religious and the nonreligious. Everybody got what they needed.

When they lowered my casket into the ground, I still didn't have a reaction because I could swear that that was somebody else's body. I still didn't feel the need to crawl back into it or take care of it. It was completely—forgive me—dead to me. Even though I didn't have any emotions, I could feel my family's solemn sense of finality. I did feel really bad for my brother, Lukas. It would be awful to carry your brother's casket, which he had done. Despite the pain, actually putting me in the ground gave them closure, at least in some small measure. For me, though, it was a release, like, "Now it's about to start." It felt like it was a new beginning. I didn't know of what yet, but I felt like something was about to start.

After my burial, I was still receiving everybody's words and wishes and emotions. There was a shitload of grief and a shitload of curiosity. People wanted to know more. The rest of the thoughts that filtered across my consciousness were just stories and memories. It was like I was strolling down somebody else's Memory Lane. I was still focused on all that instead of stuff like, "Where is my fucking bright white light? Where's my big steed that I ride off through the Pearly Gates on? How do I get out of here?" Well, let me tell you guys right now: I didn't fly off into some tunnel of light on the back of a majestic steed. What actually happened was way cooler than that.

I never thought about things like Heaven or Hell much when I was alive. My family never talked about religion. I guess that's because

my mom's parents were atheists. My family in Norway didn't share
their religious beliefs with anyone either. They just went to church for
things like christenings and weddings, so I don't think they were really
into it like the people who go to church every Sunday here. I heard
about this kind of stuff from my friends and other sources, though.
I also heard that people who off themselves end up in some sort of
purgatory or a place with, like, fucking fire and brimstone, so I was a
little worried that I'd end up there.

Those thoughts made me think about my mom. She was always
the one I went to when I needed comfort, so right after the funeral, I
followed her around the house, trying so hard to get her to see me. She
didn't right away. In the evening, she headed down the hall to my room
with Michelle close behind her. I think they just wanted to revisit the
place where I was alive last. I guess they needed more closure.

Just as Michelle was moving from the game room into the bedroom hall, I whispered in her ear, "Dude, fucking see me." Right
after I said that, her gaze seemed to change, like she was thinking,
"What's up? Is that you, Erik?" Then she grabbed her digital camera on the table nearby and started taking pictures of my mom just
as she started to round the corner of my bedroom door. She said,
"Mom, I feel Erik. He's here!" They both got all excited and scrolled
through the pictures on Michelle's camera, and sure enough, there I
was. What they saw was a bright ball of light with a long tail, kind of
like a comet whizzing behind my mom. A star was born. They were
talking about how the tail made it look like the ball of light was moving, and, fuck, I was! I could feel myself moving around the room,
just like I had at the funeral and when I died. That's the first time I
realized that my family couldn't see me in human form, which made
sense, I guess, but I still didn't really consider myself a spirit at that
point because I didn't know what the fuck a spirit was supposed to
look like. When I saw that picture, though, things started to come
more into focus for me.

Besides the whole thing when I visited Poppi to say good-bye, seeing the picture of that orb was the first time my mom felt I might not really be gone. This was the start of her journey from skeptic to believer. It was a fucking long one because she's stubborn. I don't think she wanted to believe I was still "alive" because if she did and then found out it was all bullshit, it would be like losing me again but forever. That'd really suck. Anyway, that whole experience gave me hope too. I didn't want my relationship with my family to end in disbelief.

After Michelle took that picture of me, I knew I was going somewhere—I had no fucking clue where, though. I'd heard it's called "crossing over," but I didn't feel like it had happened yet. I just felt like it was coming and that it was going to be good and that everything was going to be okay. I wasn't afraid. I didn't think I had to do something to start the process either, like wave some dead-dude flag at the big guy in the sky or stick out my thumb for a lift. I just knew that it was going to happen the way that it should.

4

Crossing Over and Meeting Loved Ones

·····

So I'd said my good-byes, my body was taken care of, I'd processed all the thoughts and emotions that were coming at me, and I didn't really know where else to go except back to the house. I focused on going there, but instead of just showing up like I did when I thought about going somewhere, something totally different and unexpected happened: I felt myself moving. It was a weird sensation. It wasn't like my feet hit the floor one after the other. It wasn't like I felt the wind blowing across me or the scenery passing me by like you'd expect if you were moving forward. There were none of the usual visuals like you'd get when you're driving in a car or walking down the street. This kind of disturbed me. No, it's more like it alarmed me because I wasn't expecting it. Where the fuck was I going, and was someone pulling me there? Was it some sort of weird-ass force of nature, like a giant magnet or maybe some sort of being with a huge cosmic fishing pole?

Then I felt this airiness like you'd feel on a roller coaster ride right when you come over the peak and drop. I felt stuck in that moment. My stomach, or what used to be my stomach (it's hard to explain how bodily feelings get felt after death—it's a bit like phantom limb pain, I guess; you still feel feelings, it's just that your actual body's not around anymore), felt like it was being lifted up, and a weightless ease filled me. My thoughts—this consciousness that was rolling through my head that made me aware of what was happening—were also coming from my chest, which wasn't what I was used to. As humans, we designate stuff like, "Our thoughts are in our head, and our emotions are in our heart, and our heart is in our chest." My emotions and thoughts were both in that unified central location in my chest, and as I was being pulled, the emotions I mostly felt were curiosity mixed with nervousness.

Everything seemed to happen quickly, like a blink—a long casual blink, like when you're tired. Suddenly, I felt warm, like I was in a really nice warm bath, but the warmth was all over me. I felt it on the inside; I felt it on the outside. I was absorbing the warmth, but I wasn't breathing it in. Well, I wasn't breathing at all, since spirits don't need oxygen, but you get the idea.

Then I saw white light around me. Yeah, you do see a white light—no fucking joke—but it's not like the white tunnel of light people expect when you "cross over." It was like I was moving across this huge white room with a white floor. For some reason, the light comforted me. It eased my nervousness a little bit, but not all the way. There were no smells or sounds, though, and I didn't see anyone. I thought there'd at least be some angel playing a harp on a cloud, but no—just silence and whiteness.

For a while, I just focused on what was around me. My thoughts then wandered to my physical form. It *felt* like I had arms and legs, a head and a chest, but I didn't. I wasn't solid. I was airy, free, light—the essence of me. Now I know that I was pure energy, but I didn't call it that back then. I think the reason I felt like I still had a human form but also knew that I didn't was because I wanted to have the feeling of a human body. I wasn't 100 percent ready to let go of my human existence then. I needed something recognizable to hold on to for the time being.

Slowly, the white light started to turn into this glowing silvery mist with all sorts of beautiful hues that I don't even know how to describe. It was like I was going through a nebula but with a rainbow of many colors. I didn't feel like anything startling was about to happen, like I was about to be hit by a train, but at the same time there was this little lingering worry that I was going to end up in the wrong place, kind of like Harry Potter when he's getting sorted by the sorting hat. Everything was too much, too close, too crazy all of a sudden—that's what made me scared. It was then that I screamed for help.

After I screamed, I started to see shapeless blobs in the light. Things started to change around me again. My logical mind said, "You moved," because I was still trying to think linearly, but it was more like a dimensional shift. Energetically, what happened to me was that I was coming out of the human dimension to enter a parallel one. Later, I learned that dimensions are all parallel but kind of smushed and swirled together.

The blobs of light turned into what looked like people. So many people. I thought they were people, but I wasn't sure. Maybe I was in Heaven and they were angels. Maybe I was in Hell and they were devils. Either way, they fucking freaked me out. Think about it: My only memories were from my human life. Seeing that dimensional shift and transformation was like watching a scary movie. Shit turning into monsters like in that movie *The Blob*. It spooked me.

With those "people" around me, I felt like the center of attention, but it wasn't an ego thing like, "Look at me. I'm all that." Once I realized I wasn't in a horror movie, I actually started to feel love. That transition from being spooked to feeling loved was like seeing somebody in the dark and not knowing who they are and then getting closer to them so that you get a better clue, and then the fog lifts and you're like, "Hey, man. What's going on? You scared the crap out of me." The love I felt was the kind that brings you to your knees, weeping. Happy tears. Tears that wash you clean. I was *that* important. I found out later that all that love was necessary to begin my healing process. It's weird because in human life, sometimes the more people there are, the more expendable you feel. You're like a piece of meat. Here, *everybody* is important and no one is more important than the other. Still, I was afraid that I'd never see my family again. I was afraid that I'd be stuck with these dudes I didn't know.

Next, I noticed that there were two "people" around me. They weren't shapeless. Instead, both of them looked like they had human bodies, and I think they looked like that so I'd recognize them. They were helping me out with all this new dead stuff. One of them was Aunt Denise. Like me, she'd killed herself, but she did it by overdosing on her pills. She had been very sick from having diabetes for years. Her kidneys didn't work; she couldn't walk without help; she could only eat through a tube; and she was almost blind. In a way, I couldn't blame her. I wouldn't have wanted to live like that.

Aunt Denise was in front of me, to the left. Hers was the first smile I saw. That was when I had this awakened moment that this was *really* real, even though I sort of thought it might be before. Now it was different because I was about to have real conversations with dead people. (It still hadn't really sunk in yet that I was one of them, even though it was pretty obvious that my physical body was dead.) I asked her if I was in Hell, and she laughed and asked, "Why? Because I'm here?" Then she hugged me. She was so happy, and I was confused as to why. Isn't that funny? It was like I didn't catch what made her happy, and I didn't realize it was because of me. She was happy to see *me*. She was happy to *be with* me. When she hugged me, I hugged her back. After that, there was no talking for a while. Everything was quiet and peaceful, and the white light I'd seen before was still shining. It seemed to be brighter behind her, and I still felt warm.

I knew there was a woman to my right, but I didn't turn toward her. I was still focused on Aunt Denise. Then the other woman stepped forward and gave me a hug. That's when I recognized her as my grandmother—my dad's mother, Bestemor. Other than my mom, I've never known anyone as sweet as her.

Aunt Denise took my hand and walked me forward, explaining what was happening to me and telling me that everything was going to be okay. She made sure I kept moving and told me I couldn't go back. I had no problem walking with her. I didn't hesitate at all. I was wondering where the fuck she was taking me, but I wasn't nervous about it. I got the feeling that she was taking me to a place where something important was going to happen, but I can't tell you why I knew it. Since the other voices and emotions I was trying to manage from the funeral had faded away and I wasn't processing all that anymore, it felt like I was gaining my focus back, and I was just focused on her.

Just like before, I didn't feel like anything was moving past me as Aunt Denise walked me forward, and I didn't feel like I was covering any ground, but I still knew I was going somewhere. It felt like I was in one of those dreams where you're running but not going anywhere. When I looked ahead, I saw that the white light had grown really bright. It was so bright that I couldn't see anything else, but it didn't hurt my eyes and it didn't bother me. There was such a sense of trust and peace knowing that none of it bothered me. If a light like that had come toward me when I was alive, I'd have gone, "What the fuck? Alien abduction!" but it wasn't like that.

Even then, it hadn't completely dawned on me that I had crossed over, because I thought that meant crossing some line or walking through a door. The whole thing felt like a journey where everything I experienced seemed to happen all at the same time. I had no desire or need to fight or resist what was happening to me, even though I didn't know where I was going and what the fuck was going on. It just *was*, and that was so fucking awesome.

As we walked, at first all I could see around me were beings in that bright, bright light. It was during this walk that I realized these beings weren't human looking. They looked like light with a shape to it, and sometimes they morphed into different shapes, something no human could ever do. That's when I realized that they were spirits, not people, and that if *they* were spirits, then I must be one too.

When my mom and Michelle captured me in the photograph looking like an orb of light, I just figured that that was the way the camera caught me. Up until that point, I had only seen spirits represented in a human form, so it was a little confusing. Some of the spirits were skipping, smiling, and messing around. If I saw people acting like that on Earth I would have thought, "What the fuck have these people been smoking?" It didn't feel fake, though; it felt natural to me. Authentic.

After a while, my surroundings changed, and I started seeing some stuff I had seen on Earth and some that I hadn't. So this gets a little bizarre, but bear with me here; I promise it's super cool too. Imagine a very Disneyesque landscape but even more colorful and vibrant. There were lampposts and walkways and things like that. It kind of looked like a park. I also saw all sorts of creatures that I've seen on Earth, like butterflies, but these butterflies were different. They had long colorful trails behind them. It was like they were leaving rainbows in their wake, and the rainbows were shooting out sparkles like you'd see in a Skittles commercial. It was bizarre, but kind of cool too.

As I was walking along, spirits would come up to me and say, "Go this way. Okay, now go this way." They were all smiling and pointing in one direction or another, and I ended up in this really open area that looked like a utopic version of Earth. My surroundings were beautiful. They filled me with what I can only call joy. I would discover later that it's our natural state to be fulfilled here, and we create this fulfillment for ourselves.

Let me try to explain what I mean by that.

We create whatever we need in each moment. So, like, here I could be friends with the butterflies that were flying all around me, but in human life, I'd be like, "Oh. It's a butterfly. Okay," and move on. I'd never think to be like, "Hey, Mr. Butterfly, let's be friends," because that would be dumb, but here I can, and it's the most natural thing in the world. I can interact with anything and anyone I want because everything and everyone is connected, and this all makes for feeling fulfilled, and I somehow knew this intuitively from the moment I got here.

During the walk with Denise, I met all the dogs that I had had as pets growing up and started talking to them as if they were human beings. Every pet owner's dream, right? They knew what I was saying too. It was like my words got translated into a form that they could understand. I learned later that there's a universal language here that everyone speaks. It's a language of energy, and it's instantaneous. Whatever I needed to communicate to anyone here was understood immediately.

As we walked, the light that was still pervading everything all around us had gotten brighter and brighter. Denise took me into a space that was kind of like a room. I felt like I had crossed through a doorway into yet another dimension to get to that space. She brought me over to a crescent-shaped table with six spirits behind it. What followed was like an emotional communication. I really don't know how to explain that better. Later I found out that the room and the table were totally my own creation. Not everybody gets the "team behind the table" thing—I'd created that visual setup because it just seemed more realistic to me to be addressed by elders who knew better. Each spirit creates the version of their transition that resonates best with them, whether they're aware of this or not.

I thought it was a little weird to see that there weren't any lines of spirits like you'd expect to see at the Pearly Gates. I was just being presented. I didn't recognize these spirits, but I knew they weren't there to judge me. Even so, I felt like I was standing up in front of a class, about to give an oral book report, and I had no idea what they were going to do and what was going to happen.

The six spirits were tall, and the closer I got to them, the more intense their energy felt. I think their tallness and their strong energy are metaphors for their wisdom and the experiences they've had, but they didn't make me feel like they were better than me. We all have certain skills—both in our human and in our spirit forms—and these beings' skills were wisdom and compassion. I could just feel that wisdom oozing out of them, and this drew me to them. I knew that they were the ones who could help me understand what was going on and what was about to happen next.

Before we get to what happened next, though, I want to explain something to you guys. For all of you who'll cross over—and that's all of you—it's all about what you make it. What I'm trying to say is that how you get into Heaven (or whatever you want to call it—it's Heaven for me, so that's how I refer to it) will be based on the belief system you maintain while you're alive. For example, if you think you're going to go through some big-ass tunnel and be absorbed by a great white light, that's what'll happen. That's what you'll create for yourself. Same thing if you believe you're going to open your eyes and see your loved ones right off the bat. Other people think that when they die, they'll finally get to chill out because life's been so hard on them, so they'll get a shitload of rest before anything goes down.

A lot of people wonder what happens to atheists after they die, including atheists. If you're an atheist and you believe in the whole "ashes to ashes" thing and think that when the lights go out, that's it and you just disappear, then you'll simply cross over into blackness— nothingness. If the blackness is where you want to be and how you find your peace once your physical body has died, then that's where you'll stay. However, some atheists who enter that blackness may have thoughts like, "Where am I?" or "Where's the light switch?" They might realize they don't want the permanent blackness, so they'll call for help, and once they do, they cross over to the place I'm in now.

I crossed over the way I did because I didn't have a structured belief system of what would happen after I died. I didn't think that there was nothing after death, though, and that's why I didn't cross over into darkness. I'd figured that something would happen to me after I pulled that trigger, but the only thing I knew for certain was that it was going to be different and it was going to be better. I think not having any idea of what the fuck would happen was why I didn't cross over right away. Instead, I hung out for a few beats first, which gave me time to say my good-byes. Once I'd done that, it was like my crossing over just happened to me, as if some invisible force yanked me across the finish line.

It's different for everyone, though, and so is the rest of your transition, which is where we're going next.

II

....

My Transition

5

My Life Review

....

O nce the table of six spirits had shown up, I knew that I had entered
the next step on whatever this journey was that I was on now.
I was a little scared, but I also felt ready. They told me that I was about
to enter my life review. My immediate thought was, "What the fuck
is that?" It wasn't like they rolled out this scroll and said, "Welcome,
Erik. Here's how this is going to go down." There really weren't any
verbal instructions because the spirits didn't have voices. They seemed
to transmit thoughts straight into my head, and those thoughts felt
very supportive. The spirits told me that during my review, I was going
to be shown things. I wasn't given the option to do or not do my life
review. I was just told it was going to happen and that it would help me
understand who I was and how to forgive myself.

I didn't even realize that I was looking for forgiveness until they told
me I'd be shown how to look for it.

The table had a screen on it that I could look down on, but I could
also see everything 360 degrees around me. Then the table changed
shape, morphing into what seemed like one of those theaters where

the screen wraps around you, but it wasn't like I was sitting down in a movie theater, staring straight ahead at a screen, eating popcorn and drinking a Coke. As I was contemplating this whole setup, something unexpected happened. All of a sudden, everything from when I was a tiny, tiny baby to the moment I died—the good, the bad, and the ugly—came flying at me from all directions.

First came my birth. I felt myself being squeezed out of my mom. I felt her joy and her pain. I felt my family's excitement. What followed was intense, to say the least. As my entire life unfolded before me, I was not only experiencing every single moment I ever lived but I was also observing and feeling what everybody else in my life went through in reaction to whatever I said or did to them. I felt their joy, their hurt, their disappointment—shit like that. I saw their reactions to when I lied, when I withheld my feelings, when I didn't help someone who needed me, when I was mean, when I gave too much and when I gave too little. I also got to see and feel all the good things I said and did too. Seeing how everyone chose to interact with *my* choices was fucking powerful. Not only could I feel the emotions they had in response to my actions but I could actually see things from *their* perspective. It was like I *was* them. I got everything down to the smallest little detail, like how many times that person blinked and how many times they swallowed in their lifetime—all experienced simultaneously. That's how detailed it was.

I wasn't in control of the review. I couldn't change it, and I couldn't fast-forward or rewind through any of it. I wasn't thinking, "Oh, you know what would have been better? Let's hit the rewind button and watch that nice thing I did when I was five again and then skip through that shitty thing I did when I was fourteen." Nah, it just came at me. Man. I would have paid to have had that ability while I was alive because I probably would have navigated through my life differently. It's the most powerful experience that you could ever have because whether we're dead or alive, we crave an understanding of our choices. I got that with my review. I didn't ask for it; I just got it.

One of the great things I remembered during my life review was when I was given my first motorcycle, a dirt bike for motocross racing. I couldn't have been more than nine or ten, but that was the time I knew my mom and dad really trusted my abilities. They knew that no matter what situation I came across, I'd be able to handle it. That was a huge moment for me. I was so proud of myself.

The other memory in the review that made me happy was when I became an uncle. I got to go back to that moment when I held my niece, Arleen. I was afraid of holding someone so small. I was scared that I'd drop her or hold her the wrong way. I thought, "Why would they trust me to hold her?" because to me, I wasn't someone I'd trust. I looked down at her and realized how tiny she was and how big my arms seemed in comparison. She didn't even cry. She was just so happy to be in my arms. It was the first time I cried tears of joy.

I remember really clearly one time when I was kind of a dick to a friend. He was jerking me around a little bit. He'd tell me to come over but wouldn't be there, or he'd tell me I was his friend but not step up when I needed him. So I let him have it. It wasn't physical and I didn't call him names or insult him; I just said some mean things. I lost my shit because I couldn't see that all I had to do was walk away. After I blew up at him, that dude was never the same. If I had handled the situation differently, maybe things would have been different between us or he would have turned out differently. Now he's afraid that the things he says might cause him to lose a friend in the same way he lost me. Fear is what keeps him in line now, and I wouldn't wish that on anyone.

During the review, I learned that that friend bullied me because he himself was abused and beaten down. It wasn't my intent to do the same to him. Even though I was just putting him in line for the shit we were going through, it triggered that part of his past. You never know how your words or actions might affect someone. It was fucked-up intense to feel his sense of belittlement, fear, and inadequacy firsthand.

He felt small, but he didn't show that on his face, so I never knew. With my review, I was able to see his authentic emotions, his authentic self.

From that part of my review, I learned that responsibility is never only on one person's shoulders. It's meant to be shared. Yes, I had to be accountable for the things I'd said to my friend, but I couldn't be responsible for how he reacted. *He* had to be responsible for that.

My life review made me feel like I had been cast in a role and played it, and when it was over, I got to read the reviews, knowing I was just a character in the play that was my life. It's weird. It's not like I thought, "Bro, give me a red pen, I gotta make edits to that character," because I knew that whatever choices I'd made were just a part of that play. As a human, I was playing myself. As a spirit, I truly *am* myself, and I'm looking back at the part I played.

During my review, I started having these epiphanies of exactly who I was through the role I played. All the questions like, "Why did I behave like that?" "Why was I a dick to that person?" "Why did I make that decision?" or "Why was I nice to that person?" became part of the bigger picture of what and why I was here to learn. These lessons were all related to my intent, whether it had to do with something constructive or destructive. For instance, let's say one day I decided to stomp on a bunch of ants. That might be a lesson for me to understand that ants have feelings, and by hurting the ants, I also hurt myself. We all live as a collective—animals, plants, humans, all living beings—so the lesson I would have gotten from killing those ants would be that we're all connected, and when we hurt others, we hurt ourselves. Every action has a reaction. Those kinds of epiphanies during a review can be very profound. They definitely were for me.

My life review also allowed me to see every possible outcome for every choice I'd ever made in my life, and, as you can imagine, the possibilities are infinite. For instance, if I hadn't consoled my sister, Michelle, when she had a bad breakup with a boyfriend, things might have played out differently. If I had been an insensitive prick instead, she might have ended up in bad shape, and I saw that if she and I hadn't been so close, my niece might never have been born. Every single moment is affected by every other moment. Life is like a long, twisting line of dominos, and our choices dictate which ones fall where.

Throughout my life review, sometimes I would drop my head down on the table and cry, and other times I would fling my head back and laugh, but I never felt judged by those six spirits, and I never had that feeling that I'd done something wrong. It's weird to explain, but that was the first time I understood that there *is* no right or wrong. I wasn't feeling judged because there *is* no concept of judgment or shame here. I looked at each moment, each experience, for what it was—a valuable lesson, no more and no less—so I had no need or desire to fix or take back anything I'd done.

When you're alive, you usually live by a set of morals and values and parameters that you either set for yourself or that society or religion sets for you, and that's mostly a good thing. In general, people need codes of ethics to live by in order to function in society, and those codes often dictate how we react to situations—with joy, with fear, with shame, with anger, and all that stuff. Here, it's not like we're lawless beings running amok, messing with shit just because we feel like it. No, it's more like we've transcended concepts like right and wrong, good and bad, and all that, and entered a plane of existence outside the definition (and the need for the definition) of concepts like that.

Anyway, at the very end of my life review, I came to the moment when I died. Even though I knew no one was judging me for taking my life, I kind of cringed inside because I knew how much pain it was causing for the people I love, but that feeling of non-judgment comforted me. That's when I started to forgive myself. That forgiveness would become one of the biggest parts of my healing.

How long did my life review last? Two seconds? Twenty-four hours? I really don't know because there's no linear time here, but everything seemed to happen in an instant. Think of those movies where visuals flash by really quickly. (What's that called? A montage?) It was kind of like that, but even that's linear, just at a fast frame rate. I got a sense of everything in one quick flash—an instant download from beginning to end.

After my review was all over, there I was, still in this white room. That's when the six spirits explained to me that the purpose of exposing me to what I'd just witnessed was to gain something from my experiences as a human. They also told me that, whether I knew it at the time or not, I, along with the other spirits that had crossed my path, had designed everything in my life. My life had been about creating contrast. For example, they told me that in order to completely learn about forgiveness, I'd had to betray myself or someone else. In order to learn the value of relationships, I'd had to go through some shitty ones or not have many at all. It was a rough way to learn important lessons, but that's the way it was meant to be for me, and I see that now.

Man, there's so much that happens in your life review. The main thing I got out of it was that deep understanding of right and wrong. Like I said, you're no longer ruled by "right versus wrong" guidelines, and there's no self-judgment like there is in human life. Without that judgment, I was able to forgive myself. Like I said, that was definitely the most powerful part of my life-review experience.

After it was over, nobody really took my hand and showed me the way out. It wasn't like some movie was over. No curtain closed, I didn't walk down the aisle with popcorn sticking to my feet, and I didn't have to wait in a long-ass line for the bathroom. Instead—*poof!*—the space started to disappear pinhole by pinhole a thousand times—a million times—until it just kind of evaporated altogether. If I could have still held my breath, I would have.

I wondered what was going to happen next.

6

The Blackness

....

Think of the color black. Black like the night sky when there's no moon out. Black like a black cat on Halloween. Are you thinking about it? Good. Now stop, because that's not gonna get you even close to the all-consuming darkness that surrounded me when I left my life review.

I should have been terrified, but I wasn't.

Believe it or not, it had a smell to it. If I had to describe that smell, I'd say it was like the fragrance of crisp morning air. Then, slowly, these colors started to appear out of the darkness that surrounded and permeated me. I've never gone deep-sea diving, where it's pitch black except for those creatures that can create their own light through bioluminescence, but that's what those colors were like. They were their own contained light source. It was beautiful.

The blackness was like being in a womb before you're born. I guess it's kind of also like a spiritual car wash. It heals you, nourishes you, and prepares you to go on to the next step in your spiritual existence all new and sparkly clean. This part of my healing didn't take very long for me because my energetic field wasn't all that damaged, despite the fact that I'd committed suicide.

I feel like that's going to be hard to understand for a lot of people, and believe me, I get it. No one should have to feel so bad about living that they want to escape it at any cost, but sometimes that's just how things shake out. The only way I can put it, and as simply as possible, is this: no judgment, and infinite forgiveness. I know I said this before, but I wanna be really clear about this: that was the biggest aha moment from my life review, that right and wrong are human constructs, and what really matters is forgiving yourself and others. It boils down to compassion and love.

So, yeah, for me, my healing felt more like a car wash: I put my quarter in at the beginning; I got my wash, which was my life review; I got air blown on me to dry me off; and I went into that darkness, where my energy was buffed and mended.

You might wonder why everything was black. I did too. Well, the thing is, I had to go through blackness because up until then, like after the life review and everything, I had focused all my attention on myself and what created the dark, unhappy life I had lived. I had to experience that darkness for what it really was before I could release it and be healed—just energy, not good or bad, but still all around me and inside me.

Before I go on, I really want to say a little more about living with a mental illness because it's something that heavily influenced the way I thought and acted when I was alive and, in a lot of ways, continues to influence me as a spirit. Living with a mental illness sucked for me because I was always second-guessing myself. And no matter how great I felt one day or week or month, I'd always plunge back into severe depression and hopelessness.

My mental illness made me feel like I was wrong and everyone else was right. It made me feel like they had something I didn't and that they were living their life in a certain way that I wasn't—or couldn't.

It's like everyone but me came into life wearing the same size shoes but my shoes were two sizes too small, so I had to walk through life in pain.

Anyway, what all this talk about mental illness has to do with the blackness is this: as I spent time there, feeling myself being washed clean, all the stigma and pain and confusion of my disease fell away along with everything else, and for the first time pretty much ever, I felt what it was like to be free from that.

During my time in the blackness, my "body" started to feel different too. At first, I was afraid (I was petrified! Haha. Sorry.) to look down on it, so I didn't. At that point, I just felt that I didn't have a sense of human anatomy or shape anymore. It wasn't like, "These are my fingers; this is my nose," and I didn't have that feeling that my skin was the boundary between my environment and me. I just got the sense that I was some sort of light with a shape to it, maybe like the beings I'd seen earlier. Then that dark healing space pixelated away pinhole by pinhole again, and I decided to go for it and take a look at what I was made up of now that I'd crossed over.

7

My New Body

....

Eventually, I found the courage to check out my new body. When I did, I realized that I couldn't find my dick. Ladies, I'm sorry if this doesn't resonate with you, but I have to say it. If you're a dude, you get it. That's the first thing a guy would wonder about. It's just how we're wired, and some of that physiological wiring, I guess, got carried over into the afterlife, at least initially. I noticed that I didn't have any limbs either. That's when I recognized that my body was different.

Really different.

Imagine dropping your chin to your chest and looking down at your abdomen, your legs, and your feet. When I did that, I saw this massive collection of energy swirling around a core, almost like a small universe. There was some kind of gravitational pull that kept this energy all collected in and around itself to create whatever shape I wanted at the time, and for some reason, I must have wanted to look like a stick. No arms, no legs, and, like I said, no dick. Somehow I knew that this new body was my true, authentic self, though. You might call it my true essence.

My energetic body felt numb, but it wasn't the same numbness you'd have in a human body. It's not like when you sit on your leg or fall asleep on your arm and you get pins and needles. It was more like the way I would feel if I were in a dream, and that "dream self" doesn't have any feeling. Now I realize that this numbness was because I hadn't accepted my new form as being real 100 percent yet. It was just something I had to adjust to, like everything else.

Eventually, I tried to move my stick-like energetic body. When I moved through this space I found myself in, it wasn't like I extended my energy and popped out a leg to put down on the ground and move myself forward. It kind of felt like I was surfing a wave. It was kind of like coasting or gliding like a hovercraft.

I also noticed that all the small things we do unconsciously when we're alive, that I had done as a human, like breathing, wiggling my toes, and blinking, no longer seemed necessary. I also wasn't feeling any craving or needs or desires. I just existed, pure and simple. That's when my humanness really started to fall away from me, like crumbling ash stuck to my energy. Not all the way, but most of it.

8

My Senses and Emotions

....

At first it didn't dawn on me that my senses were also different. I don't experience them the same way as I did when I was a human. I can create different senses based on my memories from my human life, but I can also experience them separate from those memories.

Taste was the first thing I realized had changed. I had this memory of having a mouth—you know, like putting the pizza in and experiencing the sensation of taste—but it's different from that now. I recognize that I have taste, but it's not like a taste that's just stuck on my tongue. After all, I don't have a tongue! My energetic body can merge with the energetic field of someone on Earth who's eating a pizza, and I can taste what they taste, but it's not the "food on tongue" sensation. I taste it all over and inside my spirit body. I can also taste the pizza if I merge my energy with its energy.

Delicious, delicious pizza energy.

As for my sense of smell, everything smells clean and fresh here. It's one of those other things that's hard to describe. Not to disparage pretty much everyone on Earth, but language kind of sucks. You guys need more words! Anyway, it's the same as with taste. All I have to do is merge with an energy field to smell something—like, I can go up to a flower and merge with its energy, and I experience its smell.

As for my sight, I see 360 degrees, which is kind of cool. When I manifest things with my thoughts (we'll get to more on that in a bit; it's rad), not only can I see them in my head but I can also envision them from different perspectives. I can see myself in it, around it, above it, below it, or whatever. On top of that, I get all the information from everything I see, so that gives me a sense of all-knowing that's deep inside of me. I got a little overwhelmed at first because I could see everything at once—and I mean *everything*—but eventually I learned to narrow my focus to see one thing at a time and put everything else in the periphery.

Sound is more like a vibration, and my body resonates with whatever frequency the sound vibrates at. I don't hear things like a human would because I don't have ears. I just absorb the energy with my entire body, and it can change the way I feel, physically and emotionally. When I say "physically," I mean the sensations in my energetic body.

Did you know that Earth makes its own sound? I can hear it, and let me tell you, it's fucking cool.

The sense of touch is different here too. You don't bump into someone on the street. There's no bumping and bouncing off of things here. When two spirits touch, their energies merge to create a unique energetic field. When I touch another spirit, it doesn't feel like human touch. We're like two pieces of Jell-O that kind of melt and mush up together. That was a little hard to get used to, too, but now it's kinda fun.

If I created hands and legs and sat down to rub my knee, my energetic hand on my energetic knee wouldn't feel like a heavy hand on top of a bulbous knee. It would just kind of feel a little buzzy. It's not like sticking a finger in an electrical socket, though; it's more like a vibration. I get the same sensation no matter what I touch—an object, another spirit, or myself—but it comes with a different form of consciousness. So, like with all my senses here, I gain all the information about whatever I'm sensing too. When I touch other spirits, I get their thoughts, their emotions, their intentions, and all their stories—past, present, and future—and in that moment, I'm sharing and exchanging the deeper levels of myself too. There are no secrets—no privacy—but that's not a problem here.

When I touch an object on Earth, I know everything about it, like where it's been and how it was made. The same thing happens when I touch humans too. That doesn't happen when humans touch something. They just focus on the touch itself. They don't get to know anything else about what they touch. On the flip side, I don't get that solid feeling humans get when they touch something. That's why being human is so fucking fun. The solid sense of touch is one of the things I miss most about being a human on Earth.

I also miss the kind of relationship I had with my family while I was on Earth. When you spend all your life with a group of people, it's hard to adapt emotionally to them not being there in the same way, physically and emotionally. Yes, I have connections in Heaven, and yes, I can connect to humans on Earth in many ways, but I miss the earthly physical interactions, the conversations, and things like that. Can I give you a piece of advice real quick? Hold hands, man. Hug everybody. Have a hugfest.

The best way I can explain how all the senses work here is this: Imagine lying down, blindfolded, and someone rubs something up and down your skin for you to identify. Remember doing stuff like that in school? I do. Anyway, say they rub a feather, the eraser on the end of a pencil, a rock, or a piece of carpet against your forearm or maybe your fingertips. It registers in your brain that it's hard, soft, scratchy, or whatever. Humans have descriptions like these for all their senses, not just touch. Sweet. Salty. Loud. Soft. Stinky. Aromatic. As a spirit, those senses don't register. I don't get just one sensation on my fingertips, on my skin, through my eyes, ears, or nose, if I had those. Every sensation is all over and in me. What's also really cool is that all these senses overlap and get jumbled together. When I see something, it comes with a taste, a smell, and a sound. Kind of like how synesthesia works for people who have it. When I hear, taste, feel, see, or smell something, I get a symphony of other sensory input as well, and when I clap my hands together, I can actually see the sound waves coming out.

Just like the senses, emotions are different here. I can't hold on to negative emotions. I've actually tried (maybe just because I was so used to it), but it takes too much effort. It's like trying to hold on to slippery dishes in the sink with big-ass awkward dishwashing gloves on. You just can't do it for very long. Emotions are not such a mystery here like they are on Earth. Heaven is like a naked beach, no bathing suits necessary— no covering up emotions, no lying about how you feel. You're naked, and you love it. When I was a human, I'd get sad, but I wouldn't always know why. It'd be a mystery. And if someone asked me if they could touch my motorcycle, I might go, "Yes, please touch it. Go ride it," but inside I'd be feeling, "Fuck no! Don't fucking touch it!" The other person couldn't possibly know that, but here I know exactly where my emotions are coming from and why they're there.

One last thing: Here, my emotions aren't just mine. They belong to everybody. My emotional reactions belong to every spirit, and theirs belong to me. That was kind of scary in the beginning because that was a lot to handle after keeping a lot of my emotions bottled up for so long when I was alive, but now it just feels like unconditional trust and love. It's awesome.

9

My Therapy

....

Rewind a bit, back to my Soap-'n'-Shine Infinite Blackness of the Soul Car Wash. After I was done and was just sort of float-ing around, starting to get a feel for my new spirit body and senses, more spirits showed up. They weren't the same ones who'd guided me through my life review; I felt that they were different and here for a different purpose. They led me to this table in the middle of another white room. The table was really smooth and made from a material I don't think we have on Earth. There were three spirits to my left, four to my right, and one in front of me who was doing most of the talking by transmitting thoughts directly into my head, which is how most spirits communicate. Even though things' physical appearance are really fluid here, it was as if my heart knew who they were and that they were okay. I felt safe.

These spirits said they were going to help me purge some things from the life I had just left. I thought that we'd gotten that all taken care of with the spiritual car wash, but I was wrong. There's a lot of stuff you need to sort out when you cross over, and there's no rushing things.

The spirit at the table who did most of the talking was named Cawli. It's kind of silly of me to try to describe her because it's only my perception of her. Even calling her female isn't entirely accurate because that's not really how gender works here, but she felt female, so I referred to her that way. I knew she wasn't human, but I was more comfortable seeing her as one. She's really just this light energy, but in my perception, I saw that she had long bright blond hair pulled back from her face, and her eyes were blue. She had no makeup on, and even though she looked like someone around my age, she spoke like she had the wisdom of someone who's a hundred.

Cawli had this sweet calmness about her, and her movements were slow, relaxed, and confident. She was like a gentle river that constantly moves, and I felt comfortable with her. She looked at me and asked me how I felt, but somehow I could tell that she already knew the answer. I told her I felt okay but that I was a little confused and nervous. She assured me everything was going to be fine.

First Cawli walked me through what happens at the point of death. She told me to imagine a hand filled with these glittery granules of salt, and these granules are sprinkled into the physical body when you're born. That's the life force, the soul. While the granules are in the body, they can make it move and react like a puppet. Then when you die, it's like shaking all those granules out. She said that I'd had my "Erik salt" shaken out of me, and I remember thinking that was a really funny metaphor.

Cawli helped me adjust to my death because she knew I had a problem grasping everything that had been happening to me since I passed. She began by throwing some questions at me.

"What is the definition of 'real,' Erik?" she asked.

I didn't have an answer for her, so she continued.

"As long as you are observing something and participating in it, it's real, whether there's a physical body attached to that observation or action or not." She knew I thought that she was super attractive, so she went on to say, "You look at me, and I'm pleasing for you to look at. Would you define how you look at me as real?"

"Well, fuck yeah!" I said, because I figured I might as well be honest.

"Okay, then," she responded, "it's as simple as that. You see something; you have a reaction to it. Then it's real."

She went on to tell me that just because a body dies, it doesn't mean that you no longer exist. That helped me accept that I truly was still "real" even though I'd shed my physical body. In other words, she helped me understand what the definition of *real* is, whether you're a human being walking around on Earth or a spirit like me. Cawli then confirmed something I'd been wondering about ever since I transitioned—that I was made up of some sort of light energy now and that the body I had left was just a shell, a car I'd driven around to navigate my way through all my experiences as a human. She also explained that soon after I died, I traveled through different dimensions: first after I left my body, then when I crossed over, and then when I went to my life review.

Because I'd taken my own life and on Earth that was considered a bad thing to do, I wondered if Cawli would fuss at me about it, so I was anxious about what she was going to say next. She must have sensed my concerns because she went on to tell me that there's not a term here for suicide. That's because the way you get to the afterlife isn't important. It's just a death like any other. Actually, it's more like a birth. Whether you come in headfirst, by cesarean, or feetfirst, it's still a birth. What matters most is how you carried your emotional heart when you were alive. She explained that this meant how emotionally honest you were with yourself and others in your life. One of the things she praised me for was that when I was alive, I was honest about who I was and how I needed to be, even if it pushed other people away and even if it caused me pain. Because of that open honesty, I carried my heart on my emotional sleeve, even when those emotions were hard to carry.

Cawli spoke to me with no judgment—only love. She never once used words like "good" or "bad" with me, and it didn't feel like she was trapping me in some word game like I felt some of my human therapists sometimes had. I guess the main thing that made me feel like I wasn't being judged was that she didn't treat my suicide as a taboo like many religions do on Earth. She didn't treat it as if it were bad; she just treated it like a fact, and that was very freeing for me.

Next, Cawli helped me answer some of the "whys" of my time on Earth and what they meant. We talked about why I'd chosen to come into the life I had.

"That's a complicated word, 'choice,'" Cawli said. I remember her smiling kind of like the Mona Lisa—like she knew a secret that I didn't and she wanted to share it, and I'm really glad she did.

I learned from Cawli that choices here are, in many respects, the same as the ones that humans make, but in other ways they're really different. We all make choices. We can choose an apple instead of an orange, a yes instead of a no, one career over another. You know what I'm getting at here. But there's also a form of choice that souls make that's kind of above the concept we understand on Earth as "choice"—the choice to be born into a loving family or an abusive one, for example. This isn't a "choice" that any human child could ever make for itself, obviously. You don't choose to be born with a certain hair or eye color; you don't choose to be born with a genetic predisposition for high blood pressure or addiction—but your soul does choose certain paths that you may or may not be aware of when you're alive as a human.

Say a child is born into a loving family but also grows up struggling with bipolar disorder, like I was and did. That's because my spirit chose to walk that particular path, and then as I lived out my life, I was presented with various choices I had control over that were influenced but not predetermined by my soul's path. That may seem like the absence of free will, but it really isn't. I had the freedom to live my life, and

I also had the freedom to end it, but it all led to the place I am now because that's what my soul needed.

You can learn from joy *or* pain—frequently both. Some learn compassion by being exposed to terrible hardship, and others learn it from being exposed to nothing but joy and ease. Some never learn from life's experiences at all until they're done living. I guess I was a little bit like that. I'm glad I now have this opportunity to give back some of what I've learned, though.

After Cawli explained to me how choice works, she went on to tell me what my soul had been searching for during my time on Earth and why that mattered.

"Erik, your soul wanted to learn about relationships," she said. "Relationships are the richest and most important things souls can experience on Earth, and going through everything you did with the people you went through it with helped you understand human life more, which will be invaluable for you here."

Man, was she right about that.

We also talked about why I'd picked certain people to be a part of that lesson. I'd chosen the parents I had because they would help me understand my lessons better and provide me with a safe and loving environment to do so. I could have chosen parents who were assholes, but that wouldn't have helped me personally understand human relationships as well. It would have discouraged me from forming connections, not only with other people but also with myself. That wouldn't have helped me understand love. I also chose to come into a bigger family because that presented me with more varied relationships to learn from.

In that same conversation, I also started to understand the separate roles I played with my father, my mother, and my siblings when I was alive—the lessons that they learned through me, I guess. For example, with my mom, my death was supposed to help her accept the fact that she couldn't heal me. Life with me as her son was hard for her because all my issues were dumped into her lap. What made things worse was that, in spite of her being a doctor, she couldn't heal her most important patient: me. My death was a hard lesson in grief and separation, but it also set her on her own spiritual path of healing and acceptance.

Cawli talked about how my mom's healing and spiritual growth would help me find my own feet in the afterlife. I didn't know what Cawli was talking about at the time, but she said that together, my mom and I both would become the best versions of ourselves. That's what we signed up for. Of course, what Cawli meant was the fact that my mom and I would start communicating with each other through spirit translators and go on to do awesome shit like help heal the rest of our family, aid lots of other people with their journeys from skepticism to belief and from grief to joy, and even write this book.

Cawli also showed me how my bipolar disease helped me learn about relationships. The stigma of having a mental illness had made it hard for me to have relationships with other people. It scared them. They couldn't understand me. They didn't want to, and that pushed them away, so it was hard for me to make friends. This helped me understand why people react the way they do. During therapy with Cawli, I felt their fear, and through that, I developed compassion for them.

Cawli showed me how being mentally ill also created a wall between me and other people because I was holed up in my own little cage, trying to deal with my feelings. Being alone in that cage made my family try to find the key that would set me free, even though ultimately that was not in their hands, and that was okay. Their efforts showed me how important and healing some relationships can be and that you can't go through life carrying your burdens on your own.

Another thing I learned from Cawli was that I wasn't supposed to connect to anything strongly on Earth. That's another reason why my soul chose for my body to have bipolar disease. It helped me maintain the distance I needed to detach myself. One foot in one world, one foot in the other. She told me I had chosen that kind of existence so that I would have the courage and strength to leave early.

We talked a lot about why I had died so young. When you take your own life, it's often viewed as one of two things: cowardice or negligence. Either you're a coward for not "trying harder" or whatever or the people around you weren't with it enough to notice the signs and stop you from going through with it. I guess that both these things could be true in certain circumstances—no judgment; that's not what I'm here for—but for me, it wasn't about that stuff. It's not like it was my destiny to take my own life or anything like that, but the way I took my exit did have a lot of impact on many levels for a lot of people—and not all bad—so in a way, it was the right choice for me.

When someone young kills themselves, it's looked at as particularly sad, and that attracts a lot of attention and makes people ask a lot of questions. My death made people—including my family—ask things like, "Why couldn't he have been healed?" "Why couldn't he have gotten older and wiser?" The answer to that is simple: I didn't need to be wiser. I needed to get out. My brain wasn't working the way that I needed it to in order to participate fully in an earthly life. I'm now living a much fuller life than I ever could have when I was in my body. Again, this isn't to say that people shouldn't fight to live with everything they've got. They totally should, and man, I did. I'm just saying that I'm okay with how things turned out for me personally.

Cawli also told me that my early death was supposed to have a big impact on my family by showing them the true value of relationships and love. It taught them that they can't assume that if people they love are young that they'll have a lifetime together. Now they know that everyone needs to nurture their relationships with those they love because you never know how long they're going to be around.

My death was loud. It was like a scream, and that made it even more painful for my family than it would have been otherwise. It made me realize how much I could hurt other people, and it made me want to do the opposite of that, which is, I hope, what I'm doing now.

One of the most interesting answers to the "why" of all the pain and suffering I experienced in my life as Erik I didn't figure out until much later, but Cawli planted the seed of it during our first therapy session. Eventually, I figured out that I was supposed to be a guide and help humans, and the compassion, empathy, and listening skills I gained during my life were important for me to become a better one.

When I crossed over, I didn't really find out that that was going to be my job here right away. No one tells you when you cross over what your job will be. Cawli didn't tell me out and out that I'd be a guide, but, like I said, she gave me clues. At one point, she said, "You are such a blessing because the experiences you've had can be a guiding light for others." That was the biggest seed that would help me put two and two together down the road. Every answer to my many "whys" came down to the spiritual contract my soul had picked for itself, and that was to learn from my own relationships and experiences and then use those experiences to come here and become a better spirit in the afterlife.

. . . .

At one point in my therapy, Cawli said, "Erik, now we're going to look at your other lives."

Um, what the fuck? My one life was more than I could deal with. There are others?

It turns out that I did have other lives, and not only did we discuss those other lives in detail but she also explained their connections to the life I knew as mine. The one that influenced my last life the most was when I was a monarch butterfly, because I had these stages to go through: larva, caterpillar, cocoon, and then a butterfly in flight. There were transformations in that life, both physical and emotional, that taught my soul a lot about growth and change.

It was such an incredible journey exploring my life as a butterfly, flying from one country to another—the struggle, the excitement, and the community. In my life as Erik, I wanted to have that but couldn't. I was stuck. My body and my mind were broken. I think that when I was human in my last life, my soul wanted that same energy from my butterfly life, but it just didn't shake out that way. Revisiting that life helped me understand a lot of feelings I experienced during my life as Erik.

In another life, I was this woman in France in the 1400s. In that life, I didn't have a lot of money or anything, but I was wicked smart, especially when it came to growing plants for food. I found out that the best way I could help people was to teach them how to save seeds and exchange them for crops. I worked with the local monks outside Paris who knew that the soil had certain properties and that some plants grow better when they're planted after other crops. Because of this seed-sharing thing of mine, I was able to help so many people who couldn't grow food for themselves. That life was so awesome to explore. In it, I felt good in my body, and I helped others in a way that I had wanted to in my life as Erik, especially people who were having a really hard time. When I look back, I see how that life was meant to influence my existence as a spirit guide whose job it would be to plant the seeds that humans need. But I don't want to get ahead of myself; I'll tell you guys about being a guide soon.

Revisiting these two lives and so many other ones and being shown their connection to my "Erik life" gave me a sense of wholeness I'd never known before. It helped me see the common thread between all my lives—and that was my emotional pain. In most of my lives, I developed compassion for others through that pain. I knew that if they felt the pain that I did, then they needed as much compassion as they could get.

In some of my lives, the pain was a product of my being given more responsibility than I could handle, and that almost always resulted in disaster. In others, it was because of the death of someone important in my life, like one of my children. Those really made me sympathize with my parents and gave me a better understanding of their grieving process and their emotions and thoughts in general.

I think the biggest source of emotional pain came from those lives when I was disappointed in myself and in my relationships. That often made it hard for me to let people in or it made me push people away. Either way, learning what a relationship *shouldn't* be helped me learn what it *should* be, and because each relationship is a mirror of the one you have with yourself, every one of them helped me understand why I was the way I was as Erik. Knowing that the people and my relationships with them made me "me" dissolved a lot of the mystery that made me feel incomplete. At the end of my first discussion with Cawli, I was left with a sense of relief because I knew that all that pain served a good purpose.

. . . .

My therapy with Cawli caused me to have a lot of epiphanies. One of the biggest was that I'm an amazing person and I have a really big heart. I think that when you're on Earth, living your human life, revelations like that are sometimes viewed as self-centered or egotistical. No, man, love yourself! I wish I had been able to tell myself, "Dude, you're fucking awesome!" more when I was alive. Another big aha moment: Cawli told me that I was more in control of myself than I'd ever imagined when I was a human. My bipolar disease made me feel like I wasn't in control when I really was, but now I know that even that was my choice. I wasn't some pawn on a chessboard. I was in control the whole time. I wish I had known that before I fucking died. Still, putting things in perspective sort of healed a part of me, even if it happened after my death. I found out that I wasn't powerless. I had the power in me all along, and I just had to find it.

In all our conversations, Cawli never used words like "hardship" or "struggle." By showing that my soul had picked to live the life I did as Erik for a reason, she reminded me that there is no right or wrong. Everything is just a lesson—one that, even after death, I'm still learning.

There was one thing Cawli said that I had to figure out for myself, though. It seemed like I could only stand by helplessly as I watched my family on Earth cry and grieve, and I didn't know how to comfort them, heal them, and tell them it was going to be okay. I would eventually figure out ways to help, but Cawli gave me the emotional support I needed to get through those feelings of frustration and confusion in the meantime.

At the end of my session with her, Cawli told me that most of my therapy was finished, but she wasn't going to leave me stranded. She said I could call on her anytime I needed her, and that was a relief. I met with Cawli from time to time after that first therapy session, mostly to just go over stuff that we talked about the first time in more detail or whenever I was feeling like I could use some clarification or a reminder. I know Cawli and I will always be friends. Here, each time you connect with someone in spirit, you merge with them more and more. Relationships get a little bit deeper and broader as you become more intimate with their energy, so my connection with her gets stronger and stronger. It's nice knowing that someone's there for you when you need them, and Cawli's one of those someones for me.

Cawli still helps me when I have trouble feeling something with my heart. Sometimes I need a little coaching. She shows me how to tap into a wealth of information, using my heart instead of my head, and that takes learning how not to think. Whenever I start to think with my head, she says, "Erik, focus on your heart. Look at what you're trying to process as emotions, not thoughts. Every experience comes from an emotional place. Emotions create the thoughts, and thoughts create experiences." I remember one time she said, "The cup that holds knowledge is the heart, and the mind is supposed to take sips from it. Everything starts from the heart. Everything starts with a feeling." I think that that's one of the most important things I've learned from

Cawli. I also think that that's probably one of the most important things people living on Earth should know and pay attention to. It's definitely something I wish I would have done more of when I was alive. Listen to your heart because it knows what it's talking about.

Even though I don't have a physical heart anymore, I still listen to my heart as a spirit. That was a huge takeaway from my therapy with Cawli. With the information I get through that process, I can continue to grow, but the growth that happens here is not about learning something new. It's about reconnecting to the information that was there all along but that maybe you couldn't see or access when you were alive. My growth now is more about how I'm going to absorb the knowledge and experiences I already have. It's about whether I'm open to a new perspective and whether my hands and heart are big enough to hold it.

10

My New Perspective

···

S ince my life review and my therapy, my perspective has changed.
Instead of being egocentric, where all my awareness is on *me*, every-
thing feels geocentric because all the focus is on everything *around* me.
This makes me feel an incredible connection to everything.

Let me explain it this way: When I was human, chilling in a park,
I'd think, "I'm in a park next to this oak tree." Now I'd think something
like, "That tree is near the playground, and the playground is in the
park, and the park is in the city, and the city is in . . ." You get the idea.
That'd make me feel a connection to the tree, the playground, all the
other things and people in the park, and the space in between them
instead of how the texture of the bark felt against my fingertips, how
the waistline of my pants was bugging the shit out of me, or that I was
playing hooky so I could have a smoke off the school grounds.

Being geocentric instead of egocentric doesn't mean you surrender
your identity completely just because you feel like you're connected
to everything. You can acknowledge your identity, but you can also
acknowledge that the space around you has equal value to you. Imagine

walking down a street and there are people holding umbrellas, traffic lights changing from green to red, cars passing by, and buildings all around. Now imagine arrows pointing from you to every life force— every animal, tree, whatever's alive. These have the same value as the "I." Instead of "I am moving forward," it's more like "I am moving in unison with all this."

Most people can feel that for fleeting moments, but if you work on it, you feel it all the time, whether you're a spirit or a human being. That means you have to change your language and the way you think. Humans usually have egocentric language. They think, "I'm sitting behind a desk," which emphasizes that the most important thing is you and your location related to the desk's. If you broadened that view, it'd be more like your presence in the environment as part of a whole. You could see yourself in the south side of the room instead of your specific location in association with the desk in the room. You'll be aware of the space of the room rather than the item in the room. Then the language is going to change. You'll be like, "The desk is in the southern part of the room," instead of, "I'm sitting at the desk."

The shift in my consciousness also switched from my head to my heart. My head isn't running the show anymore. There are no thoughts racing around in my head like, "Did that shit really happen? Yeah, that really happened," or "Oh my God, is that girl looking at me like she likes me or like she thinks I look like an idiot?" It's so weird how I don't rely on just the thoughts in my brain anymore. I mean, I don't *have* a brain now, but I'm just using that word to explain what I guess I'd call "head consciousness." Now my entire body communicates in a different way. It's through my heart. It's hard to explain, but my heart can now communicate independently from the voice in my head and has this whole conversation in and of itself. I'll call it "heart consciousness."

Heart consciousness is hard to define because it's so nebulous. It's easy to grasp head consciousness because you can hear that inner voice in your head, word for word. As a human, it was what I was used to, but this new type of consciousness is more emotional. Now I lead with my heart. I lead with my emotions. I feel first and think second. I feel an emotion, then that triggers a thought, and then that determines the choices I make. As a human, I had it all backward. I had a thought that triggered an emotion, and then the emotion caused me to act or react in a certain way.

That shift to heart consciousness helped me heal by letting my heart take the front seat to my head, so that my negative thoughts don't get in the way anymore. If I had to give that heart-centered consciousness a sensation, I would say it's like that much-needed sleep after you're physically, emotionally, and mentally exhausted. A deep, healing, relaxing sleep.

When it comes right down to it, I think that the biggest shift in my perspective once I became a spirit was the realization that a lot of the pain I suffered when I was alive was a result of not listening to my heart and my emotions and letting my brain run away with itself. As soon as I was able to think with my heart instead of my head, I got it. I even understood the true nature of suffering. I understood that suffering is caused by resisting what you're struggling against or stamping it down or ignoring it. Thinking only with your head makes you resist stuff.

Resistance comes in many forms. It might be looking away from the pain or denying it. It might be blaming someone else for it or trying to bury it in drugs or sex or whatever. If I had listened to my heart more when I was alive, I'll bet I would have been a lot happier, even though I would have still been sick and I know that things probably would still have turned out like they did. Maybe I would have reached out more or listened more or just loved more. All I know now is that if you use your heart and embrace it for what it has to offer instead of just using your brain to resist what you struggle with all the damn time, you're gonna be a lot better off—mind, body, and soul.

III

The Afterlife

11

My First Look at Heaven

....

Up until after my therapy, except for the short walk I had with Aunt Denise and my grandmother Bestemor, I was limited to a pretty restricted amount of space—not because anyone was keeping me there against my will or anything but because I just hadn't yet ventured out into Heaven's surroundings. After I'd taken in everything from that first therapy session with Cawli, I truly realized that I was a spirit now and this was something permanent. Once that kind of sunk in and I had gotten a handle on my new spiritual body, I decided to start exploring.

I remember when I first started to look around. I thought it was weird that I didn't meet any angels. I was looking for them, but nope— not a single feathered, winged creature to be found anywhere.

The next thing I noticed was that I was in a clearing of sorts, sur-rounded by a dense forest. It kind of looked like what I'd expect to see on Earth, like the meadow in that scene from the movie *Bambi* where his mother gets shot. (My mom cries every time she watches that part.) At the same time, I noticed big differences. Unlike on Earth, everything seemed like it was painted with vibrant colors, even the clouds in the sky. Even the air. Everything. And there were colors that I'd never seen or could have imagined before. They made the colors on Earth seemed incredibly drab in comparison. Think about the colors on Earth and multiply their intensity by ten, a hundred, a million—and not only were Heaven's colors in high definition but they were also three-dimensional. Colors here move and live and breathe as if they have a life of their own. Looking back, that is the first memory of Heaven's environment that I had.

The smells are also different than the ones I experienced as a human. They were like fresh rain. There are no perfumed fragrances or dirty earthly smells like pollution or exhaust. It just smells like crisp spring water. Still does.

I thought it was strange that when I was looking at my surroundings I only saw what I focused on from moment to moment. My perspective was different. It was as if my eyes were telescopic. When I focused on something really small or close to me, everything else went blurry. I also had these instant connections with whatever item I was looking at. I wasn't just observing it. I felt like I was one with it, sharing the same energy and source. Then I could pull back and see everything that was far away again.

After taking this all in, I looked around and saw what seemed like a nature reserve. There were huge trees that were alive, of course, but not just in the "I've got my roots in the ground and I'm growing" way. The bark was alive; there were *sounds* coming from them. If I saw that on Earth, I'd be like, "Somebody fucking drugged my ass!"

There were paths everywhere, and they weren't made of cobblestone. They weren't paved with gold. They were just well-worn dirt paths. That really doesn't make any sense, now that I think about it, because my feet didn't touch the ground. It's not like I was treading on it and destroying the grass and the tiny insects like Godzilla. Later, I wondered why there were paths, and I found out that it's because humans are used to seeing them and it was helping with my transition to envision stuff that I'd recognize from Earth.

When I broadened my view even more, I saw other landscapes, like deserts, snowy fields, coastlines, and grassy plains. These landscapes don't follow the same rules they do on Earth. There, I wouldn't expect to see a desert right next to a swamp. That would make no sense ecologically or geographically. But that shit happens here. I could be in a desert, walk ten steps in one direction, and suddenly be in a swamp.

I also saw other spirits like I did on the way to my life review. It's difficult to describe what other spirits look like because that's shifting all the time depending on how I choose to perceive them and how they choose to be perceived. When I was first exploring, the only way I can think to describe it is that everyone just looked normal to me—kind of unremarkable. It was comforting. They were doing their own thing. It wasn't like they were paying attention to me, going, "Hey, new guy!" But I still felt like they were acknowledging me in some way.

There were animals, too—forest animals like deer, birds, and squirrels. None of them seemed to be domesticated. There were also animals I had never seen on Earth. I'm not talking about unicorns and shit like that. There are just life forces that are unique to Heaven. One of the first unusual animals I saw was about the size of my hand. It was living in a tree, kind of like how a squirrel would, and was covered in lots of colors—mostly bright yellows, dark browns, and black. It had feathers, not fur; its tail was short, and its face was striped like a chipmunk's.

I also noticed that there was something different about the sky—or I should say, that space above me, because it's not really the "sky" like the sky on Earth. It didn't look like it belonged. It looked removed from the landscape, like it began thousands of miles away rather than merging seamlessly with the horizon like it does on Earth. It's difficult to describe, but the sky just feels huge here, like driving through Montana on a clear day but a million times more intense.

All the sights and sounds in this expansive landscape made me feel happy as hell, but at the same time, it overwhelmed me a little bit. It's like being on overload listening to four or five different songs at once, but as soon as I focused on my happiness and only that, all of a sudden it was like I could hear all those songs, harmoniously, at the same time, clearly and easily. Actually, it's not like I had to focus on it to get it. It's almost like I had to disconnect and accept it. That's when I stopped feeling overwhelmed and started just feeling wonderment and even contentment.

12

Manifesting Things

··

After I first explored parts of Heaven, I thought, "Holy shit. I need a place to live!" See, even though I'd pretty much accepted that I was a spirit now and that this was my new home, my mind-set hadn't fully transitioned yet. I still kinda *felt* human in some ways, especially in my thoughts. I wasn't ready to go 100 percent into spirit mode yet, so I thought myself a house.

I have a hard time describing how manifestation works here. (Yeah, yeah, I know—I have a hard time describing a lot of shit. Give me a break!) But if I had to put it into words, it's sort of like daydreaming, except that your daydreams come to life instead of just staying in your head. It's not like it doesn't take any work. It takes practice, like anything else, but it's like thinking or dreaming something into reality.

When I manifested my house, there were spirits who helped me design things based on what would make me feel comfortable as I continued my transition to Heaven. They helped me create my own peaceful and familiar little world. It's weird; I can manifest things instantly just by wanting it. When I create things, there's a thought in my head and a feeling in my chest. If I only use my heart, what I create would look really abstract. It wouldn't have a form. If I only use my head, it'd look like a plain box. Using both gives me the feeling of something abstract, but the form melds with it to create something beautiful, like a finely carved cabinet or jewelry case.

I like to work with my hands, so I manifested things like hammers and nails to build part of my house manually. I needed that, but not all spirits do. I think it ended up looking pretty good. I made the outside of my house of wood. I guess I'd describe it as a log cabin. On the inside, I made myself a bachelor pad—a dude's home. It's a two-story house with pale wooden floors. On the first floor, I have a fireplace, some musical instruments, and a bar stocked to the hilt with liquor, so it's decked out like a party pad where I can entertain if I wanted to. On the second story, I have my couch and a TV with kickass speakers. No bed, though, because I don't sleep. Spirits don't need to. On both floors I have a bunch of big windows because I like a lot of light. Oh, and it's not dirty. That's the one thing about my environment I didn't bring over from Earth, where I was a slob. I'm kind of a neat freak as a spirit! I also made sure to include some more material possessions to make my place feel more earthlike, like some video games, a skateboard, and a motorcycle, of course.

Outside my door, I have a beautiful view. My house sits on top of a hill in a remote area, and the landscape is really green. It reminds me of the surroundings around my family's little cabin back in Norway. There are a few tall trees that are pointy, like fir trees, and there's a lake off in the distance. The air around smells crisp and refreshing, like mountain air. Just for the hell of it, I created a pair of boobs by making two hills with a tree on top of each one. I thought that was pretty funny.

Now, you might be thinking, *But if he's a spirit and in Heaven, why did he need to manifest all this shit he's not gonna use, like a house, booze, TV, and stuff?* The only answer I have for that is this: it made me happy to have created a living space like the one I did, right down to the little inconsequential stuff that, yeah, I'd never really "use" as a spirit. It was still important to me at that early stage, even if it wasn't necessary. At first, what I made was based on the memories of my life on Earth because those memories were still really strong. I remembered my home, what I ate, what I wore, and what my house and my surroundings were like, so I created all these for myself and more. What's weird is that the minute I didn't need what I created, it stopped existing, and so after I got over my transition period and started really letting go of my earthly possessions, all these things just disappeared. I can manifest it back into existence, and sometimes I do, but it's not something I really need anymore.

Nowadays I don't need all those things I had as a human, so I've mostly let go of the concept of having a home and possessions. I see now that there's no benefit to having all that shit here. Sure, I can conjure up a motorcycle if I want to kick ass on some imaginary track of my own creation, but I don't need those wheels to feel connected to my earthly life as Erik. Now that I see Heaven as my new reality rather than a material one, I don't live in my Heaven-house anymore. I still have a home base, though. It's the home I grew up in on Earth, where my family still lives. It's so full of happy memories and love that I find the solace I need when I'm there. I hang out around my family's house most of the time because I like being with my mom, my dad, my sisters, and my brother.

So, back to manifestation. Thought is actually energy—like everything is—but it's easier for spirits to manipulate thought-energy than it is for humans. But like I said before, this shit isn't easy by any means. It's not like I cross my arms and blink something into existence like that genie chick on the TV series *I Dream of Jeannie*. Still, it took a lot of practice for me to get really good at it because it takes so much fucking energy to focus my thoughts on what I want to make. First, I practiced in situations where the bonds are really strong, like the one I have with my mom or with things and places I feel a strong connection to. For instance, I have a strong connection with the house I grew up in, and that bond helped me align my energy with it so that my first house could come into existence. I guess that's a "like attracts like" thing.

Here's another way to think about it: Picture the dust bunnies under your bed. First they're just little specks of dust, but over time, those dust particles pull together to make a dust bunny. Well, I have an infinite amount of energy—lots of dust—to use, so I can make anything I want. And my thought-energy sends out tendrils to find similar energies to connect to. Then I pull all that energy together to create another energetic shape. You can compare it to building a sand castle on the beach. You have all that sand available to you to mush together into a shape. Then when you're done with it, you can un-mush it so that it goes back to the rest of the sand. Well, I can mush together my energy with other similar energies to make something, and when I'm done with it, I let it go to the collective energy mass.

These days, if I create a beautiful park and a bunch of other spirits end up really liking it, using it, and thinking about it a lot, it stays put energetically. I've learned that the more spirits focus on something, the more stable things become in our world. Sometimes I work with other spirits to create something we all want. It's easier to manifest stuff along with other spirits because our energies can work together. For instance, once a bunch of us made a snow slope so we could snowboard together.

At first, when I tried to make stuff using the energy of something I didn't have a connection to, it was fucking hard. When I don't have a strong bond with whatever I'm trying to work my energy magic with, I have to create an awareness of that connection. It's not as easy as thinking, "I want a one hundred–pound bar of gold," and the bar appears. I don't give a shit about gold. I don't have a connection to it. So I have to focus and practice to create that connection. But the more I practice, the better I become at building that bond. In the case of the gold bar, once I focused that connection into existence, I could meld my energy with its energy to make it. I call that "entanglement." It's kind of a physics thing because when electrons and other particles sort of get together and do a dance (they don't really dance like a waltz, though, but you get my point) and then move apart, they still do their dance no matter what the distance is between them. Everything here can be explained with what people understand as physics on Earth, but there are different rules of physics in different dimensions and universes.

While I was creating all this earthlike crap to make myself feel at home, nobody stopped me. It was crazy. No one was saying, "Hey, son, stop that shit. You don't need it." There was no big master guru hanging over my head saying, "Nah, man, you're wasting your time!" I could create whatever I thought I needed or wanted, and I progressed—both with my abilities to manifest and with my realizations about what was important to manifest—in my own time.

13

More About
What Heaven's Like

....

I really want to tell you more about what Heaven's actually like. I don't know if I'll ever be able to fully put into words how amazing it is here, but I'm going to give it my best.

As I got to explore and know my surroundings more and more in my early days as a spirit, like I mentioned before, I came to realize that "landscapes" in Heaven look a lot like those on Earth, just sort of . . . more. Like they're amplified. Sometimes the meadows, forests, mountains, beaches, deserts, coastlines, and stuff are created collectively by a bunch of spirits, like in the case of that snow slope, but I can create my own private landscapes too. I don't always like to make them the same as the ones I used to see on Earth. There, when I saw a tree, I'd just see the tree. When I create a tree here, I make it so that I not only see it but I can hear it and smell it too. I can be and feel one with the tree. Sometimes I don't create any form at all. Then I'm just hanging out in this beautiful heavenly white light.

Besides nature, there are cities here too. I've never been much of a city person, but these are nothing like the ones on Earth. Imagine a city of light that has these beautiful, ornate spires reaching to the sky. The most beautiful buildings on Earth look really unimpressive in comparison. Heaven's buildings look almost crystalline, but they're not made of anything you might call solid. They're made of pure light.

The cities are central places where everybody can go. It's weird. All the spirits that go there are actually *part* of the cities' structure but separate at the same time. Think of it like this: Every cell in your body combines to make up your whole body, right? They're separate, but they also make up the whole. So the buildings are actually made of little pieces of light that are individual spirits who can still be free to do anything they want at the same time. It has something to do with our interconnectedness and ability to split off into several "us's." (I'll get into that a little later too.)

Like I said, we have buildings, but they're only for specific activities like learning, listening to music, holding meetings, problem solving, and a hell of a lot more. There are a lot of big-ass lecture halls where groups of spirits learn all sorts of things, like how to travel to different dimensions, how to manifest shit, and how to become effective spirit guides, to name a few.

We have libraries, too, and they're amazing! They have books filled with so much fucking wisdom, it's unreal—books where I can pretty much learn about anything and everything in the Universe—other dimensions, other planets and the beings that live in and on them, whatever I'm curious about. All knowledge can be found in those books, and all I have to do is merge with the energy of the book to get its information, and if I want to learn about something but the book containing the knowledge doesn't exist in the library, I can will it into being. I love walking into the libraries here, thinking about what I want to learn and absorbing it into me. It's a lot like downloading information onto a computer. I wish I could have done it when I was in school back on Earth. Man, I hated reading.

There are some things we don't have that are important to humans. For instance, there are no grocery stores, malls, restaurants, and things like that. Of course, we can create these things if we want to, but why do it when we don't fucking eat, we don't really sleep, and we don't need to shop? Yeah, there are some spirits who like to play the role of a chef or a grocer, and there are spirits who want to sit at a table and pretend to eat or push carts down the aisles of a grocery store or sleep on a bed, but they do these things because they enjoy them, not because they need to do them. I didn't have to build part of my earthlike home manually—hammer, nails, and all. I just enjoyed playing that role.

There aren't any hospitals here because we don't really need medical care. Instead, we have healing centers. That's where energy is mended. It's pretty much designed for people who've crossed over in a traumatic way and need some extra care as they transition. Remember my spiritual car wash? That happened in one of the healing centers.

We don't have paved streets like on Earth either. It's not like we have to get into our Volvo and drive to the neighbor's house or to the gym. We just think of where we want to go and—*poof!*—we're there, just like when I had first died and thought about going outside with my body as the paramedics wheeled me outside, and suddenly I was there. We do have paths—like the well-worn ones I saw when I was exploring Heaven for the first time—but they're more for our visual pleasure than to get us places. They're placed around the gathering spots, like the libraries and other buildings, but they're also in the garden areas.

Here in Heaven, there are different areas where spirits hang out, other than cities. Remember when I mentioned about how, if a bunch of spirits all liked the concept of a park, they could manifest it collectively and it would stay in place as long as they continued to think its existence? So, there are these locations—I guess you can call them manifested spaces because those are the closest words I can think of—that have been created by thousands of energetic beings who are fully aware of that space on a permanent basis. They don't exist permanently in the way that buildings and houses on Earth do.

I'll explain it this way: On Earth, every time a human goes into their living room, they know how the couch is arranged, how the pillows sit on it—these are permanently static until you physically move them. But here, if there are five different spirits, and each of them wants the couch they've created to be in different locations, it can shift and relocate to five different places. There are as many different scenarios as there are spirits who create it. The color of the couch might soften or brighten and then become more muted. The pillows might become firmer and then softer. The plant on the side table might be bigger and then smaller. Sometimes these can all happen simultaneously. Here, that room has a life in and of itself that's constantly being tweaked.

On Earth, humans would describe the room as inanimate and fixed in time and space, while in Heaven, things are never that way. Everything here is as alive as the spirits who create them. I find it really intriguing to visit buildings like a library or a lecture hall with a certain architecture that I helped design, only to find that every time I go in, something's been reworked or is transforming before my eyes.

The music here also doesn't come close to what I was used to in my human life. It's like surround sound, and the way it's made is freaking amazing. Different beings create their own specific sound, and they do it according to the frequency they vibrate at. If you think of it in terms of an orchestra on Earth, a group of one type of being might vibrate in a way that sounds like the horn section; another group might vibrate to sound like the string section; and another group might do the same for the percussion section. There're other sections, and each one has more musical sounds than I've ever heard on Earth. It's (you guessed it) hard to describe. But the real cool shit about the music here is that it tunes our energetic bodies; it tunes the soul and touches right to the core of it, like a vibrating tuning fork inside you. It does the same thing to humans. You ever get the shivers or cry because of music? That's what I'm talking about. But it's not immediate or as intense as it is here.

I like to go to music concerts here. As for my personal musical stuff, I do play my guitar. That's why I made sure to manifest a couple of them in my earthlike home: a Les Paul and a Fender Stratocaster. I've always been connected to music, but I like more types of music now. Each type balances certain energy patterns, which are really expressions of different emotions. On Earth, I liked music like Rush and AC/DC because it channeled my anger and other negative emotions, but in Heaven, I like all kinds of music, even the Enya-esque type. (Laugh at me if you want, but that shit's great!) And the other cool thing with music here is I can smell, hear (duh!), see, touch, and taste it all together. In Heaven, all your senses meld together, and that makes everything more intense, but not in a bad way. It's one of my favorite things about being here. Things that would have been super overwhelming on Earth are just commonplace, and I never feel like it's too much to take in or handle. As a spirit, I'm built to receive all the sights, sounds, tastes, smells, and textures that Heaven, Earth, and infinite other dimensions have to offer, and it's never gonna get old.

When I was first getting used to Heaven as my new home, I felt like I was on cloud nine. After those first feelings of uncertainty and even some fear, a feeling of joy surged through me because I knew I was in the right place. I knew I was completely connected to everything around me. It's hard to explain, but I had to adjust to absorbing all this bliss that I never could find on Earth, where I had to fight to get happiness. Here I don't have to fight. I also wondered when the contradictions were going to start again. My life was full of them. People would say one thing and do another. They'd promise me things or treat me nicely, only to let me down. As a human, I learned to not have trust in anything or anyone because not only were there a lot of contradictions but also everything good always seemed to come to an end. When I made the best meal I ever had, I ate it, and it was gone. A trip, a TV show, sex, whatever, always had an ending. At first, I reflected on how great it is here, but then I thought, "When is this going to fucking stop? When is the other shoe going to drop?" So here I am in this amazing place, experiencing all these awesome things, and I didn't want it to end like everything else always did. I remember thinking, "Please be real. Please be real. *Oh shit*. What if it's not? What if it goes away?" Now I don't have those thoughts. The joy hasn't stopped since I've been here. It's been very consistent, so I've accepted it, and I'll never question it again.

14

Living Creatures

....

The wildlife here is fucking unbelievable. Every animal that has, does, and will exist on Earth can be found here—even dinosaurs. We also have animals that can't be found on Earth, like that unusual feathered chipmunk guy I told you about. Some are from other universes, planets, and dimensions, and some are the creations of spirits like me. None of the animal spirits here are like pets. It's not like, "Oh, I have horses out in the pasture." Nobody "owns" animals here like people do on Earth. We're all equal and companions.

Personally, I like to hang around elephants the most. They communicate in a way that demonstrates their natural grounding. On Earth, when they stomp their foot on the ground, it makes a vibration that creates these flowing ripples that connect them to another elephant. It's an unspoken form of communication that they can use to help each other, among other things. From them, I've learned how important it is to be grounded on Earth, and by "grounded," I mean centered and focused as a human so that life seems to make sense. Being ungrounded makes humans feel confused, unbalanced, and directionless. I wasn't grounded when I was living as a human on Earth, which probably explains the confusion and emotional instability that caused a lot of my pain. I wish I had known that connection when I was alive, but I didn't. Even if I had, I wouldn't have known how to ground myself anyway. It's a hard thing to learn when you're going up and down on an emotional roller coaster. I also like elephants because they're big and strong but also gentle, and they have a lot of wisdom.

We have plant life here that you don't have on Earth, and we see plants differently too. I think people on Earth see plants as almost inanimate objects, even though they grow. They put them in a pot and water them, but then they're like, "Eh, it died. Okay, whatever. I'll get a new one." It's not like that here. Plants are considered to be equals. They communicate with each other through these energetic root systems, and we can communicate with them too. It's like we create these little thought bubbles that merge with each other. The bubbles are kind of like waves of energy. That's how the conversations work, and just like with human spirits, the communications are based on feelings. You know how you sometimes finish the sentences of a really close friend without even meaning to, or you can just pass a look back and forth with that person and you both immediately understand without needing words? It's kind of like that.

All spirits, including plants, animals, and insects, get the same level of respect here. They're treated as equals. They're just as beautiful and smart as human spirits are and can communicate just as well—even better. Animals, plants, and human spirits can communicate with those telepathic thought bubbles I mentioned before, because they're open. They don't have a brain that can be negative, judgmental, or analytical. They don't get worried or depressed. They don't build those walls we have that close us down.

There's this portal here where wildlife and plant life cross over into Heaven after they die. All wildlife and plants cross over in a very instinctual, organic way. They don't feel the need to plan and control it like humans do. They just let it happen because they don't have some sort of expectation or belief system about what happens after they die. When humans cross over, what they believed in life tends to influence how they experience their transition, but with wildlife and plant life, it's a free-flowing river.

One of my favorite things to do is to watch insects pass through that portal. It's like watching an insect fireworks show. Damn, it's amazing. There's a high turnover of insects on Earth so millions and millions die at the same time. Think of the mosquitos! And when their light energy comes into Heaven, they're like little sparklers. Close your eyes right now and imagine a million sparklers lit and burning, crackling and sparkling—*pop, pop, pop!* That's what it's like. It's so amazing to watch this beautiful pyrotechnics show, and trust me, I'm not the only one. There are thousands of other spirits around welcoming all that light energy as it comes back into our dimensional plane. It's like the Fourth of July every night of the year.

15

Adjusting to Timelessness

···

Adjusting to time not being linear like it is on Earth was weird. It's just that, as a spirit, I can't get myself to live in the past or focus on the future. Time stands still here. It's sort of what I like to call "stacked." What I mean by that is that in Heaven, every moment is stacked on top of each other, not laid out in a straight line. Here, time is like a big ball of yarn instead of a single straight thread. It doesn't just zip by for me like it did on Earth. I never have to check in and think, "Shit. I missed that." It was like an alien abduction moment when I was plucked out of the perspective of linear Earth time. At first, I had to help myself adjust by creating small linear experiences that I could pick and choose. For instance, I'd replicate the whole nighttime-follows-daytime cycle so I could feel like I was experiencing "normal" days on Earth. If I want to, though, I can make it daytime all the time here, which is pretty cool. You do get used to timelessness eventually, but it takes some doing.

When I was adjusting to this stacked time, I did feel disoriented and overwhelmed for a little while, but then I learned to narrow my focus so that I didn't have to see all the linear time that humans create on Earth at once. Think about riding a bike. At first you have to pay attention to everything in a sequence, like where on the pedal to put your feet, how to push on the pedal to make it go forward, and how to balance the bike so you don't do a face plant. When you have that all down, everything becomes automatic, and you're not aware of all those individual steps anymore. Now I can stuff all the other extraneous shit into my unconscious awareness so it doesn't fuck with what I want to pay attention to consciously. Everything else becomes background noise. When I focus on one point in time, all the other moments I was accustomed to as a human—past, present, or future—becomes like a whisper, something that's in the back of my mind.

As a human, you often feel like there's never enough time. Then there are moments when you feel that time drags on forever, especially when you're going through something that sucks. That's because you're giving time more power, attention, and energy than you give your own personal needs. You're letting time rule your choices instead of making those choices yourself.

For example, look at people who are really good at prioritizing their needs and overall well-being, and then ask them about their concept of time. I'll bet that, yes, they look at their watch to make sure they make it to that three o'clock meeting, but they also don't let it control or ruin their whole day. Say they're five minutes late. They don't let that make them feel anxious or guilty; they just roll with it and make up for it as best as they can and then move on. They don't freak out and consider themselves a failure or get frightened that they're going to be fired. They relax in their car and think, "Just relax. Everything is going to be fine." So they're a little late. Big fucking deal.

If they're really late, it might be because traffic was all backed up. It might be because they needed the extra sleep after working on a project until three o'clock in the morning to make sure it was perfect for the meeting. It might be because their kid was having a meltdown and needed comfort and an extra-long hug. In those instances, they're serving their personal needs. These are the people who behave in a way that fulfills *them* instead of letting the clock run their lives, and those are the people whose energy will reflect this inner peace they've made with the passing of time, and then that energy will reflect outwardly onto their interactions and relationships.

I learned, once I was dead, that time had shaped a lot of my life: The clock alarm rings; I wake up and then go to school. The bell rings and I go to the next class, and several classes later, I go home—and the sequence went on and on in a continuous loop. Sometimes that stressed me out when it didn't have to. Yes, there were times when I was doing something I loved, like putting lifts on my truck so it'd be four inches taller. That's when I was in the zone and time seemed to disappear; it became meaningless. Those were the times when I paid attention to my own needs instead of what the clock said. I think that's the one piece of advice I'd give to people on Earth about time: You're in charge of it, not the other way around. You just have to remind yourself to treat all time the same, whether you're rushing to a meeting or participating in your favorite hobby. It's all just time. If you adopt that perspective, I think it'll show in really positive ways in your life.

16

Help with Adjusting

··

You know that Beatles song that goes, "I get by with a little help from my friends"? Well, it's the same here as it is on Earth. Adjustment takes time, and it's easier when you've got support.

All through my transition there were spirit guides around to help me out. One was my Aunt Denise. When she was a human, she was clumsy like my mom, but when she became a spirit, she realized that clumsiness was all about her not being centered. After a while, she became steadier. When I tried to adapt to things after I got here, there was a clumsy feeling to it, so she gave me pointers on how to make my adjustments smoother and more stable. At first I felt like a dancer tripping over my own two feet, but with her help I've learned most of the moves and stopped stepping on my partner's toes—or mine—as much.

That's just an analogy. I hate dancing. Anyway, Aunt Denise taught me through conversations, visuals, and one-on-one spiritual instruction. She comes and goes now, stopping in whenever I need to talk with her or ask her a question or vice versa, but in that first transitional time, she was such a huge help to me, and I'll always be grateful for her.

There was also this one guide who never left me during my transition period. Sometimes I knew he was there, but I didn't see him. That was a little creepy, but I got used to it. Instead of talking to me with words, he just used the flow of energy that's inside and all around us to teach me. When I had trouble or needed to ask a question, my thought energy flowed to him, and then he fed the answer back to me through the same energetic channel. Think about the times when you're waiting at a stoplight and you get that feeling that the dude in the car next to yours is staring at you or when you can feel someone's eyes on the back of your head. That's an energetic connection of sorts. Here, you get that same hairs-standing-up feeling, but instead of just a feeling or sensation, you get a bunch of information along with it. Spooky but cool.

Let's use another example. Let's say, as a human, you're happy and you don't even know why. It's not like you were thinking about something nice; you just suddenly get struck by a wave of joy. If you find yourself thinking, "Hmmm, where did that come from?" wonder no more: that's your spirit guide sending you love and support, and you're slowing down enough to feel it in that moment. Spirit to spirit, it's very similar. My guides give me this vibrational lift, this extra energy as a gift that makes me feel comfort and strength and security in the knowledge that everything's okay. It's pretty sweet; you get sent informational energy through your whole being—*Wooosh!*—all in one moment.

_17

Traveling

....

Traveling is different here. Of course, you can think of Venice and suddenly find yourself there because of that whole "thought creates reality" manifesting thing we've got going on here, but it's partly about changing your energy as well. With my thought energy, I can change it to a more earthbound frequency, an astral frequency, or the frequency of another dimension, universe, or planet, and that's where I go. I have a whole new passport, and it'll take me anywhere I want to go.

Early on, I preferred to travel to quiet places where there are soft rolling hills, still water, and not much else. It's like I was drawn to these serene, calm spots because they were clutter-free zones. My mind at that time was still disoriented, so I needed peace and simplicity in my environment to be healed and balanced, a place where there wasn't a lot of noise or distractions. Now I like to go to places that help me learn. I've actually gone to places where there's a lot of chaos and disorder, like this one dimension that's full of junk and smoke and there are physical things that all of a sudden morph into what I guess you'd call on Earth a form of antimatter. There are no earthlike rules of physics there to keep it ordered. Going there helped me learn to be comfortable with the randomness of things. When I was alive, I was always ill at ease with chaos because the muddled noises in my head made me uncomfortable. Since then, I've learned so fucking much from contrast, and I appreciate it now while I didn't before.

My primary focus is going to Earth. That's where I really enjoy spending my time. One thing I like to do is travel to the Earth's vortices—where the energy gathers at particularly strong points. I like these places because the way the Earth moves its energy in these hot spots is refreshing. It's like the difference between swimming in a dirty pool and a clean one. The energy in these vortices is extremely clean. It comes from the heart of the Earth so its vibration is very different. It doesn't really take me anywhere, though. It's not like I jump into a straw and get sucked into the heart of the Earth. It's more like a pull that holds on to me, and I love to get right into the vortex points and stay there for a while, just relaxing. Sorry to be a little crude, but it's exactly like pressing my face between two lovely breasts and resting in their warm softness. Humans are really attracted to the areas where these vortices are too, but they really can't explain why. They just resonate with the human life force so that they sleep better, feel better, whatever. The Earth is so awesome. I'll never get tired it.

I don't have to just travel to outer spaces; I can travel to inner ones too. I figured that out as part of my job as a spirit guide, which I'll get into a bit later. Sometimes when a human has some sort of issue that I don't have, I need to make it an issue for me so I can understand it enough to help them. I don't mean this literally, but I get into the mind of someone because the mind is the door to that person's own little universe. Everyone is their own little universe. So when I do that, I can see what's going on in their life and what's creating what they identify as a dysfunction, and when I help them, it helps *me* grow.

Here's the crazy shit: when you go into your own inner universe, you realize that there are other entities in it that are inside *their* own little universes too. Isn't that wild? It has to do with us being part and whole of a collective. The best way I can describe it is by looking at the human body. I'll use the same analogy as when I described the city of lights here: There are trillions of cells that make it look like one big-ass body, but each of those cells is its own little life force, its own little universe. Universes inside universes. Fucking amazing.

When spirits travel to Earth in an energetic form, they get to travel through time and space, but since I'm an energetic body, I'm still bound by energetic systems or laws. Humans, on the other hand, are bound by gravity because they're in that dimensional plane. It's similar for me as a spirit. I still have limitations based on how my energy can maneuver and where it can go. For example, when I travel to other multidimensional planes to visit other multidimensional beings, there are certain protocols or rules I have to abide by out of respect. Just because I'm a spirit doesn't mean I have the freedom to go anywhere and do whatever the fuck I want. You know, I don't get to come to Earth and scare the crap out of people. I can if I want to, but that sense of respect keeps me in check. Plus, I don't want to scare anyone anyway.

One of the main reasons we don't run amok is because we want to protect people's experiences of being human. If spirits were all up in humans' faces all the time, their current incarnation would have no meaning. They'd feel like they're still connected to the spiritual realm, and that makes it hard for them to go about the business of life on Earth. It interrupts the lessons they're there to learn. None of us want to be the noisy, obnoxious kid that interrupts class to get attention. That's not what being a spirit guide is about.

18

My Spirit Friends

....

I didn't have a lot of friends on Earth—at least not genuine friends—but I do have them now. When it comes right down to it, we really don't have labels of "friendships" like "best friend" or "acquaintance" here because we have that energetic connectedness, so everybody is my friend. There are no strangers, but it's not like I go, "I'm going to hang out with *everyone* in Heaven." I tend to attract spirits who have the same kind of work, the same kinds of hobbies and interests, or the same kinds of thoughts that I do. Most of them are spirit guides like me (I promise, for real, I'm getting to that!), and we talk about our work a lot.

I like to do a lot of different things with my friends here. Sometimes, I'll just sit around and have a pretend beer with some of them. Yes, we can conjure up a bar, and yes, they have lots of beers on tap. Sometimes I like to participate in different sports. For example, I snowboard with this kid, Antal. We make it our regular thing. I've even gone surfing on the sun! It's so much fucking fun, and there's no need for asbestos jumpsuits or an admission to a hospital burn unit afterward. Occasionally a friend or two will go motorcycle racing with me, but I usually like that to be my solo thing.

Some of my friends love nature like I do, so we create places where we can enjoy it in all its glory. We go on hikes either here or in other dimensions or planets that have completely different landscapes. We also go fishing. Personally, I like fly-fishing because it's difficult, and I like a challenge.

All these friends who like nature-related activities here usually had issues getting grounded on Earth, and, for me, being ungrounded as a human gave me a lot of grief in social situations. That's the great thing about nature, though. No matter if you're in a forest or by the sea, scampering across sand dunes, or climbing a snow-covered mountain, nature helps you get grounded. Everybody, go hug a tree. Walk barefoot in the grass. Look at the night sky. Seriously! Nature on Earth is extraordinary, man. Appreciate it.

Anyway, back to my spirit community. I also have a girlfriend named Jillian. I didn't have many romantic relationships when I was a human; I could count them on one hand. No, one finger. Anyway, she's really hot, and she's my soul mate. It's kind of embarrassing to write about this stuff, but I want to be honest and not hold anything back. When Jillian and I first met, I felt like I've always known her. (Sounds cliché, but it's the damn truth.) I'm so comfortable with her now that I want to have her around me all the time. We didn't have to go through any courtship phase because, like I said before, spirits know everything about each other, including what they're feeling and thinking. Jillian and I know we want to be together. I'm really grateful for that because I've never been very good at begging.

Our relationship is a beautiful one, and it continues to evolve. All that relationship drama that happens on Earth doesn't really happen here. Eventually, we became so comfortable with each other that we wanted to dive deeper and go to the next level. The way we did that was by merging our entire energetic beings—every bit of me felt every bit of her completely—total immersion. It was like nothing I'd ever experienced before. I remember the first time Jillian and I had sex. How could I forget it? And yes, spirits have sex, but not in the way that it's done on Earth. With sex between spirits, there *are* no boundaries. During the experience, Jillian and I shared everything: our thoughts, emotions, all our lives. I felt totally vulnerable but in a comfortable, safe way, and that takes complete trust. Vulnerability on Earth often implies weakness. In Heaven, it's not like it takes strength or anything. It's just a natural, open state of being.

When we had sex that first time, Jillian showed me how to look beyond the physical aspects of sex, and by physical, I mean the energetic creation of physical sensations. You can have those same sensations that you have on Earth, but they're more intense. Think high-definition sex. There's no resistance either. I'm talking about the resistance you'd feel when you hold someone's hand. Everything is wired between us. You know how when you have sex and the orgasm runs up a few parts of your body, and it feels totally awesome? It's like that for us, but it extends throughout our entire being, and it's not limited in any way. It travels beyond the energetic body and shines outward, and it doesn't last for only five seconds or something like it does on Earth. There's no biological limit on it. It just keeps expanding and soaring. It's complete connection, and it's totally addictive.

Jillian's helping people on Earth the way that I do, so we have a common interest. She mostly concentrates on helping parents raise their kids. In one life, she tried to save her little girl who was drowning, but she didn't know how to swim, so they both died. That's why she's doing the work she's doing. She tries to guide parents on Earth to treasure their children and see how truly amazing those little souls are.

I'm so proud to know all the spirits I know here and have all the friends I've made and continue to make. There are so many more, but I wanted to give you a sampling of the sorts of relationships you make as a spirit—and, I guess, to make sure you know that love and connection and friendship don't just end when you die. It continues on like everything else.

As a human, I felt lonely a lot, but I don't feel that way now. Here, we don't have that illusion of separation like humans struggle with. Separation is what creates loneliness. Since we're all completely open to each other, I don't have anything to hide. That means I don't get embarrassed like humans do. Embarrassment triggers loneliness because it separates you from other people. I feel like, when I was a person on Earth, my thought patterns went something like this: "I don't want to be around people because they'll see who I am or what I did or what I said that I'm embarrassed about or ashamed of. Now I'm by myself, and I'm hurting. I don't know how to break this cycle." When you get into that place, you eventually start thinking, "I really want to be with them, but they don't want to be with me. No wonder I'm lonely."

Man, it's rough being a human! I guess what I'd say to people going through stuff like that is: Chances are everyone else is probably feeling the same or similarly about it, so you should throw caution to the wind and just be honest about how you're feeling and what you need. Sure, you might get hurt, and hurt bad, but if you don't try, how will you ever know?

19

Spiritual Jobs

....

Any spirits can have jobs. Like I've mentioned before, I'm a spirit guide, and I'm learning more and more skills in my position all the time. Spirit guides are kind of like taxicabs in New York City; they're really common. Some spirits are teachers, some are healers, and some are kind of the equivalent of life coaches, I guess.

It's not like how it is on Earth, where you design your life around what work you choose, and we don't identify ourselves based on our "work." It's not like, "Who are you?" and the other spirit answers, "Well, I'm a guide." It's more like: "Who are you?" "I'm Erik," and then, "Oh, and what's your passion?" "I help people on Earth learn and evolve." So we identify ourselves with what we love to do more than anything else.

Here, spirits are lucky that we don't have to deal with the necessity of working for a living like people do on Earth, so we don't have to try to force ourselves into a position that really doesn't fit our needs and passions. There's no external force saying something like, "Okay, my father was a doctor, so I'm going to be one too," or "I need to make a shitload of money, so I wanna be a lawyer." Like I said, "jobs" here are internally guided.

One big thing that being satisfied with my job as a spirit has taught me is that true passion and self-love drives happiness, not wealth or prestige or whatever. What I learned from working with humans is that when they feel stuck in any situation, whether it's a job, a relationship, poor health, or whatever, is that if they don't like it and they feel stuck, then it's up to them to change it. Easier said than done, right? Yeah, believe me, I feel you. People usually get stuck because they allow themselves to get mired deep down in ruts partially of their own making. But I really don't want to imply that you're miserable because you "choose" to get stuck with a dead-end job or "choose" to have health problems or anything like that. That's not what I mean. What I mean is, even if you're stuck in a shitty situation, job, whatever, push yourself or find the support to find the things that will bring you joy and help you make progress toward something better. Whether it's taking night classes to work toward a degree that will one day help you get a job you enjoy more or going outside to walk for a half hour every day so you can breathe some fresh air after sitting in an office all day, that stuff really fucking counts, even if it doesn't seem like it in the moment. Once you recognize these things, then that's when you start to put your energy and focus there, and that's when shit starts to change.

Of course, you also have to be willing to accept what brings you joy. Believe it or not, some people don't. They're not willing to accept what could unstick them. For example, some think they don't deserve a new relationship or a new job, so they can't imagine themselves opening up their arms to embrace it. That's the biggest obstacle for people, but when you begin to find and focus on the steps that will yank you out of the La Brea Tar Pit of your dissatisfaction, that's when the good stuff starts happening.

Sometimes all it takes is a time-out. Take a vacation. Travel somewhere, even if it's just to the next town or city. Take a break from daily life. It also might help to talk to a therapist, a friend, a life coach, or your spirit guides. But my main point is this: Through my job as a guide, I've learned so much about passion, and how, well, *alive* it makes you feel. Even if it's rough going and takes a long-ass time, find something you love to do and chase that thing, whether it's the job that makes you money or not. You could be a postal worker and then knit sweaters for, like, hairless cats on the side, and the sweater knitting is what ultimately feeds your soul. That's what I'm talking about.

20

Angels, Spirits, and Guides

S ince I've been here, I've met all sorts of regular angels, guardian angels, and archangels as well as fellow guides and other spirits. Basically, a spirit is what I am, and being a guide is what I do. All guides are spirits but not all spirits are guides, and angels are another kind of spirit on a different level than my friends and me. I'll try and explain as best I can.

The first thing you should know about angels is that number one, they ain't got wings; number two, they ain't got halos. The reason that everyone on Earth has different ideas about what angels look like is because angels, like spirits, morph into different physical and energetic forms based on how they want to be perceived. I imagine that angels appear to people a lot of the time as big human-like creatures with wings so that humans don't get all bent out of shape wondering, "What the crap is this bright ball of light hovering in front of me?" They have to appear in some familiar form so that people can recognize, "Oh, that's my angel. She looks like us, but she glows! I feel comfortable around her. I can trust her."

People also believe that angels have wings because their energy moves differently than how it does in a human body. It moves in large, sweeping movements, kind of like the big-ass wings of an eagle. That gives you the picture of these really high, arched wings sweeping up and behind them. Sometimes an angel's energy moves in front of you like the wings that reach out to embrace. You see the image of them holding you with feathered wings, not arms. Then other times their energy reaches out to their sides like a big bird showing off its wingspan, and that energy shifts all around the human. They usually do that to protect a person.

Angels have powerful energy. This comes in handy for the work they do. Think of one of those big machines that thresh wheat. They make the harvest easier than if one person uses his Boy Scout pocketknife to cut the stalks one by one. So if an angel comes to help you with whatever need you have, they use their abundant amount of energy to speed up what needs to be done and what needs to be given to you. That's why a lot of people will say, "Man, you've got an angel watching out for you!" when something really amazing or miraculous happens. Angels get shit done.

Archangels don't incarnate into any living being. They don't need to. They're pure energy clipped right off from the Source—God, if you will—and they stay really close to that infinite energy collective. That makes them very powerful. Being an archangel takes a lot of responsibility and work. Their main role is to keep the balance, and they have the power to intervene to accomplish that. They react to the free will of people whether those people want them to or not. Balance isn't the right word, really, but it's the best I can come up with. They can swoop in and make big changes that will help with anything, like wars, the Earth, and even the weather patterns. Sometimes what we consider to be devastating and wrong might actually be right for the world to experience, so archangels will intervene and create that. Yes, there are atrocities in the world. Yes, there's cruelty. Yes, there's a lot of pain, but archangels use that to help humanity see the contrast and use it to make the world a better place. In other words, they bring in harmony and chaos, depending on what will create the best balance for humanity.

Guardian angels are spirits who teach, protect, and heal. They get that power because their energy is more concentrated and vibrates at higher frequencies. Most of the time, guardian angels are assigned to one human or sometimes a small group of people who need help with a career, health, family, money, relationships, and other things. They can also intervene to save lives. It's like they'll come in and say, "I'm behind you. I'm helping you with your shit because you're at the point now where you can't do it yourself." But spirit guides like me just stand to the side and whisper suggestions to you. We'll give you all the insight, but we're not going to step in and do your shit for you.

The everyday angel's role is to observe and come to people's aid but not to the extent that guardian angels do. Unlike archangels and guardian angels, regular angels have to be invoked. They have to be invited. They have to be welcomed. You gotta let them into your house. You gotta let them into your belief system and surrender to them so they can assist you. They're also more powerful than regular spirits because they're closer to the Source but not as close as archangels and guardian angels are.

To break it down: Spirit guides are instructional. We're teachers. We can suggest but not create change in a human's life; while angels intervene when called upon. Guardian angels intervene whether you ask them to or not, and archangels usually, but not always, work on a larger scale by creating whatever balance humanity needs.

Angels and spirits also guide and help each other. For example, a group of angels came to me a while after I'd crossed over and counseled me about my destiny and calling as a guide, which was really cool. I think I would have figured it out on my own eventually, but it was a lot easier with their help, and I felt a lot more supported once

Celia—he was the angel who sort of led the conversation—and the other angels explained things to me.

Spirits of every kind communicate in this universal language that's based on feeling, not words, so it took me a little while to adjust to it. Emotions are a form of energy, and we're energy, so that makes sense. All of the spirits' thoughts and feelings sort of rotate around them, almost like a solar system, and when another spirit walks up to them, they get all that information. It doesn't have to be translated either. It's like the information is coded in energy. That also makes sense because, like emotions, information is energy too. This is how angels, guides, and other spirits communicate with humans too. You've got to open up to our energy, and once you do, we'll never shut up!

21

Meeting God

....

After Celia and the group of angels told me that I was destined to become a guide and help people on Earth, I remember going back to the first home I built, the earthlike home. I sat on the couch and started to reflect on how my family was having a really hard time with my death. They were torn apart with so much grief that they couldn't glue themselves back together. My mom and dad weren't really talking, and nobody could understand everybody else's feelings. I just wanted to know why. Why? Why did my path and separation have to create so much suffering?

That's when God came to me.

No big aha or fireworks moment. It's more like that's when the voice inside me first connected with All That Is. As humans, when you sit down at a table and talk, you use your external voice and senses to connect, but when you talk to God, you hear a voice inside and outside you. It's not like a tennis match where you bat a ball back and forth.

God, Source, Universe, All That Is—whatever name resonates most with you, really—helped me understand that, for people, the illusion of separation on Earth was just as powerful as their extreme moments of joy, that I should connect to this and allow it to be an experience that will create the result my family needed. I was trying to understand and resolve their pain, but God told me to only embrace it, that it was good stuff and something valuable would come out of it. And God was right; something important did come out of it.

I learned that God appears to us in the form we can connect to the most. I didn't have that classic belief system of some man on a throne, so if that image had shown up to me, I would have thought it was bullshit. I would have preferred to see God as a hot woman, but I didn't see it that way either. God doesn't have a gender. It's not male or female, but I'm going to refer to her as She because if I had to say, the voice I heard was more like a woman's. It was very loving, very caring.

I didn't see anyone walking on in, saying, "Hey, what's up?" but I did see this fog—no, I don't want to call it that. It was more like textured air. It was nice that She didn't come to me looking like a human. God came to me in the form of pure light and energy, so it was kind of like, "You get it. You understand. This is the Truth." God could have shown up as really anything: a telephone, a chair, a dog—anything I wanted Her to be. But what I wanted was truth, whatever that looked like.

In that "meeting," I learned that God is the energy that creates and connects everything. She's like a collective consciousness that's coming from everywhere. She's All That Is, and I feel a strong connection to Her. In that connection, there's a voice or a way of communication that helped me see that God knows me, understands me, feels me and created me. Through that voice, I also got the key to understanding why I became who I am now. I gained this self-aware acceptance. All my veils had been taken off. Receiving God's embrace, that heart consciousness embrace, gave me an awareness, not only of the value of pain but also the knowledge and information about my work that I couldn't gain when I was separated from the whole.

That voice also explained to me the nature of my energetic self as a spirit—that I'm part of the wider collective energy of the universe. Not only am I *part* of that whole but I also *am* the whole in and of itself. I'm the whole enchilada and I'm one of its bites. Remember how I was explaining how time isn't really a straight line but stacked and more like a ball of yarn? That's kind of how energy works too. We're all entwined, interconnected, and overlapping because we're all made from the same stuff.

You know how I'd like to describe God? Think about time again. Imagine that every incarnation on Earth is represented by a book. (I'll get to what this has to do with the description of God in a sec.) All the books are stacked on top of each other. Humans have only enough conscious awareness to concentrate on one page in one book at a time. That's important because to have the human experience, you have to be in the now. You can't have your head scattered in all directions, diluting the purpose of the life you're living, but all your lives are happening at the same time. All the books stacked on top of one another exist all the time, and God is the book cover for those lives that kind of envelops and holds all the pages together—the glue, the stitching, and shit like that. So it's not like you have to go far to step into that energy, but when you do step into it, you have this awareness of all your lives and all universal knowledge. It's pretty cool. When I say "universal," I'm not talking about the universe that humans live in. I mean *all* universes, all of reality and unreality. Everything.

The emotions that came over me in the presence of God were more awe inspiring than any experience I've ever felt. It was that bring-you-to-your-knees crying that filled my heart with a sense of wonder and love. It's hard to describe because this is not something you could ever experience on Earth. I felt like a small baby being held by someone who loves me unconditionally, but that feeling was magnified infinitely. On Earth, that's the closest you can get to God Energy, and I know I'll always want more.

22

My Education

······································

I've learned some pretty important things in my life, my death, and my afterlife. Most of the big ones happened after my death, like communication, manifestation, the nature of time and energy, traveling, becoming the best spirit guide I can be, and the awareness that there are no secrets in Heaven. The rest of my learning has been more tailored to my individual journey, like learning how much I should let in and how much I shouldn't. It's like I'm an energy filter.

Think of a jellyfish. You know how they open up and kind of suck in the water and then squirt it out? Well, I can open up my "filter" and make it bigger to take in more energy or I can close it down to take in less. It's like I tighten or widen my energy web to absorb more of the information or less of it, more of the emotion or less of it, emotions being a form of energy. Learning how to control this flow of energy determines how separate I am from the whole or how united I am with it. If I feel like I don't want so much independent thought or autonomy, I open up my flow of energy full throttle and sort of merge with everything. It's intense. I feel like I'm being swallowed whole because all the information is so overwhelming. Sometimes I want more of that illusion of being an independent being, though. It's not like I prefer one to the other. I just like being able to control which one I experience at a given time. It's nice having the choice.

I'm still always learning, but I like the more intimate and casual learning groups better than the big lecture-hall type settings here. I don't like to go to the formal "sit and listen" events—in fact, I've never been to one. This should come as no surprise because I never liked going to class when I was a human student. I'm part of small meet-and-greet groups in private settings—those are the ones where I feel the most at ease, and that makes me more curious to learn. Because the groups are so small, I can become involved. They're like think tanks that pull together spirits with different backgrounds and views to solve a particular problem, and the spirits who participate don't always have the same expertise.

That's not the way it is on Earth. Let's say you humans are trying to figure out how to clean up an oil slick. You wouldn't call in, I don't know, the inventor of Jell-O, right? Earth people wouldn't do it that way. They'd only call in oil slick experts, but over here, we're like, "Hell yeah, call in the Jell-O guy. Call in all the beings who can think about this problem from a different, outside-the-box perspective so we can see what they can contribute and maybe what we're missing. What twist can *they* put on the solution?" I really like that. Maybe we're so open-minded because we technically don't have brains. I've never thought about it that way before!

I also learn a lot by joining spirit communities apart from the specifically educational ones. It's a give-and-take thing, so I don't just learn; I share too. They're different than what you might find on Earth, but it's also similar to joining a chat room where all the people in it are interested in traveling. We all instinctively know everyone who has the same interests, and we connect to each other energetically. So in these communities I come across, these groups of spirits communicate with me telepathically. As we move close to each other, I sense what they like and don't like. So if I want to meet with spirits interested in traveling, we connect automatically. All I have to do is pull from this huge bank of knowledge to make that connection naturally and energetically. When I'm interested in a topic, I get that flow of information, like who's going to be there and what the location and time of the gathering is. (I'm just using the word "time" because I know you're familiar with it, but remember, time works differently here.)

One of the "chat rooms" I'm in is made up of spirits who like motorcycles, of course. All I had to do was think about my interest, and we all became available to communicate. Say, if one spirit wants to meet other spirits interested in literature, they automatically hook up too. I'm not a fan of reading, so their beckoning little energy fingers pass me up altogether.

I've also learned about different dimensions here. I always thought Heaven was separate from the earthly plane, but now I know that it's just one of an infinite number of dimensions, and all these dimensions aren't stacked; they're swirled together with each other, including the earthly dimension. So it's not like Heaven is above the Earth, like I used to think. I just had to conceptualize it that way because the human mind likes to separate, sort, compare, categorize, and organize stuff. I know lots of religions go with the whole "Heaven's up there in the sky somewhere" thing, but it's really more like all around us.

I used to have trouble with this idea of dimensions being swirled and folded into each other, but now I'm pretty sure I get it. Think of this book you're reading. There's a page on the left side and a page on the right side. Most humans think there's nothing in between those pages, while actually 99 percent of that "emptiness" isn't really empty. All the dimensions are among those pages—hell, if I really wanted to screw with you, I could put my ass between the left page and the right page right now as you're reading this and you'd never know! In fact, my ass is in a dimension that's weaving in and out of every page and the spaces between them in every universe where someone's reading a book. My ass does get around.

Anyway, sometimes another spirit might tell me about a dimension I didn't know about. It's not a conversation of words and sentences or a lecture. Instead the communication and education is sent on many levels: to my head, to my heart, to my entire energetic body. It's like an instant spirit-to-spirit download, and all the information gets transferred directly and completely.

All this makes it easy to never want to stop learning. I have so many resources at my nonexistent fingertips.

23

My Typical Day

You might be wondering what my typical "day" is like. I think I'm gonna describe it in terms of an Earth day to make it easier.

In what constitutes the morning here, I head to my family's house on Earth and hang with them. It's a great time to be there because it's my mom's favorite time of the day. Everyone's quiet and everyone's happy. When my mom picks up her laptop so she and I can get some work done, I'm there. She fucking works all the time. I don't know how she does it.

I like to sit with my family when they're eating or sitting on the couch. I want to listen to the shit they talk about. There are times when I really want to say something, but that's where I draw the line. I'm there to listen and be a quiet presence, not to make a bunch of fuss. That's why I use different tactics to get their attention that aren't super obvious. I wonder if my mom notices that there are some days when—not to get all freaky, like the stars are all aligned or something—it's so much easier for me to talk to her. There are some days when she wakes up and actually goes, "Hey, Erik." It's like she knows I'm there, and she hears me in her head. It doesn't always happen that way, but when it does, it feels really good.

Communication between humans and spirits isn't . . . what's that phrase I heard one time? An exact science? Yeah, that's right. Sometimes everything lines up and the floodgates open and it's super easy, and sometimes the energy's not right. It's all about them—humans, I mean—being in the right emotional place. We're emotional beings, spirits and humans alike. Our emotions are made up of energy, so humans have to be in that emotionally aware and open space to make it easier to communicate with spirits. It takes being more open and emotionally vulnerable. I don't mean "vulnerable" in a bad way, like you're weak. I mean "vulnerable" in a way that you have the courage to be emotionally open and honest. When you're in that state, it's easier for us to step closer to you and communicate. By "communicate," I mean whatever is best for you—hearing, seeing, dreaming, whatever form that's easiest for us to connect.

Anyway, one thing I like to do when I'm at my house is hang around my niece, Arleen. She sleeps in my old room now. When she's asleep, we play together. She's really good at getting out of her body to play around in her spirit form. One of the things we like to play is hide-and-go-seek.

I also like to hang around my brother, Lukas. We weren't really close when I was alive. We were like two strangers walking past each other in the hallway, even though we lived in the same house and had the same parents. That's different now. I spend a lot of time with him when he's sleeping because that's how he can receive me. Sometimes I can do that easier when he's tipsy after partying with his friends. After I died, he buried his feelings in a little box that he tucked away deep inside him, and I'm helping him release some of that. I'm feeding him positive energy bit by bit that his soul soaks up.

After that, I like to divide myself and visit various members on the blog my mom runs, *Channeling Erik*. I can do that because, like I said, I can be in a thousand places at once. Then I like to have some fun.

Everything I do is fun, but I mean doing more alone-time stuff like traveling to different places on Earth or to other planets, universes, and dimensions. I like getting on my manifested motorcycle to feel the speed. Like I mentioned before, I like fly-fishing and being out in nature—you know, just something for me. In the afternoon, if I'm looking at it from Earth's time frame, I like to connect with like-minded spirits to go over what's happening on Earth. I'm talking about those small meet-and-greets I mentioned in the last chapter.

Then in the evening, I like to go back to my family's home, and when it gets dark and everyone in my house is asleep, I visit blog members that live on the other side of the world like Japan, Australia, New Zealand, and other countries in different time zones. That's when I prank and haunt them—yeah, I totally do that stuff sometimes. Then, even though it's not like I need to sleep, I do take some down time to think about the blog, my spirit guide work, and my family's healing process and our relationship. I guess that seems a little weird to me still, because I never did that kind of thing before I died. These are things that are important to me now, though. Which brings me to my main purpose as a spirit: being a guide.

Being a guide is fucking wonderful. It feels so good. It's not because I get something tangible in return. I don't get rewards—brownie points or frequent flyer miles or whatever. Nothing like that. I just sincerely love the job because I'm in a position to be the self I longed to be when I was "alive Erik," even if I wasn't entirely aware of it back then. When you have experiences on Earth—especially for the first time—you learn and grow from them. I can do the same thing here, but I can also access the information I need to help people without having the experiences they've had.

Here's an example: Let's say a young girl, sixteen years old, has a dad who committed suicide. I already have the experience I need to help her understand all about losing someone that way, and I can guide her based on my own suicide.

But yeah, my point is that personally, I don't *need* experiences to grow and to share my knowledge and healing with others like humans do. Sure, it's helpful to have gone through the same experiences as some of the people I help, but like all spirits, I already come pre-loaded with all the empathy and experience I'll ever need in my job as a guide. It's pretty sweet.

I'm gonna talk some more about how being a guide works in a bit, but for now, I just really want to stress how much joy and satisfaction I get from watching humans grow. It's a gift to help someone when they need help, and I love being able to deliver that help in the way that resonates the strongest for each different person. Sometimes people understand it best when it comes with cursing or laughing or teasing, and sometimes others get it more when I'm serious or just plain loving. I deliver it in whatever way will guide them the best. In being a guide, I've really found my calling, and I feel like I'm pretty lucky that it's worked out the way it has.

IV

My Life Today

24

My Life as a Guide

....

As I said earlier, I really love my job as a spirit guide because even when I was a human, I loved helping people. The way I choose who to help has to do with timing. It has to be just right. Is that person ready to listen? Is that person ready to learn and grow? Are they asking for help, either verbally or energetically? If I have the answer they need and try to give it to them when they're not ready, it's not going to work. They won't understand it.

The most common thing I help people with has to do with death and grief. When somebody dies, the person they leave behind feels disconnected and confused. Grief is a really personal thing, so they feel alone. When they need my help, their thoughts come right to me, almost like instant messaging or texting. Then, if the timing is right, that's when I step in. I guess I'm what you'd call a high-tech sort of spirit, as I mainly use the internet to reach out. Usually, I'll first go to them in their thoughts and say, without them being aware that it's coming from a spirit, "Hey, it's time to reach out. Get on the internet." When they get online, I get them to type in certain keywords like "death," or "suicide" or "loss of a son." (Actually, I hate to use the word "loss." It's so frustrating because people don't really lose us; it just feels like that for a while.) Anyway, as they're looking for answers, my mom's blog, *Channeling Erik*, pops up. I do my best to attract them to it, whether it's the first or the tenth on the search list.

The way I give them messages is pretty cool, not to pat my own back. (Actually, I'm so patting my own back; false modesty's not my style.) It's not like an idea explodes in their head. I just stand next to them and send them energy. It's almost like sending a subliminal message that goes straight to their head. Their senses are not consciously registering that they're receiving the message. They don't hear or see anything, but their brain is processing it. That's how spirit communication works, and it's funny because after I send ideas into their head like, "Go to the computer. Search the internet, and use these keywords to find my mom's blog," they find what they need and think it's some bright idea they had on their own. That's cool, though. It doesn't really matter how someone finds me, as long as they find me when they need to.

There's this one guide who taught me how to handle humans another way. Instead of using subliminal messages or other types of communication, he showed me how to send energetic cords out everywhere to create a web. Every cord creates this pattern that brings order that I need the human to see and feel on a subconscious level. This order gives them the direction they need to take. When people get stuck in emotions, they get tangled up in the cords because they focus on the chaos instead of the orderly pattern. Subconsciously sensing this web of order helps them recognize that things aren't as random and chaotic as they might think.

Sometimes I like to use one human to help another. Here's the way I do it: I'll get one *Channeling Erik* blog member who's been there for a while, a veteran who came in with a lot of spiritual understanding or got that understanding from the things I've talked about in the blog posts. Then I'll nudge a person to the blog if they're struggling.

A lot of times, the veteran member will post a comment that's actually the answer the new member needs. All of a sudden, the veteran and newbie are connected as teacher and student, and I don't have to teach them that lesson myself. People have an endless capacity to heal each other, but sometimes they just need a little nudge to get it started. I like being that nudge.

Here, I have a story for you. This one blog member, Sarah, has been a part of *Channeling Erik* for a long time. She started out with a barebones spiritual belief system, but now she's fully on board. One day I nudged this guy to join the blog. He was stuck in life and needed some direction, so I rigged his computer so that the blog would pop up on his screen. It took several times before he would read a blog post, and once he did, he couldn't stop reading for several days, and eventually he got brave enough to tell his story in the comments section. He wrote that he wasn't sure why he was on Earth and why he was having such a crappy life, so Sarah responded. She took him under her wing and taught him the value of the human experience—a reminder to appreciate the lessons we're here to learn. She connected to him with empathy and sincerity. They ended up helping and supporting each other, and all it took was a little push (and some light hacking) from me.

Even though I mostly concentrate on helping people deal with death and grief, I also help them with other things, like how to move forward with their life if they're stuck in a rut. If I sense someone is struggling with that and I think communication from the beyond would help, that's my cue to swoop in and take the person under my counsel. I don't know what to call it. Do I call it "spiritual rescuing"? There's not really any good way of describing it. People who are extremely lost in life might find Jesus and become born-again Christians. That might work for them. It pulls them back into their lives and makes them care again. It gives them a structure. It gives them this new light and hope, but how do I say that in terms of nondenominational spirituality? It's not like a "come to Jesus" moment. I don't help people find Jesus specifically. I help them discover their personal spiritual strength, wherever that lies.

Sometimes I have trouble with restraining myself when I guide people. It frustrates me because I want to do more for them than I'm supposed to. I just want to dump the whole shitload of knowledge and love into someone's head all at once because I get too excited, but my colleagues help me stay in line. They help me find different ways to deliver what I want to teach without drowning my student. I can't just drop stuff into their brains when they aren't ready. That's not going to go over well. But I can drop hints, and these small hints can help create a larger movement toward healing and progress for them.

Being the most effective guide possible is really important to me, and I can't be that if I go in all guns blazing. Guides can *influence* humans but not *control* them. A guide is both hands-on and hands-off, and it's important to know which tactic to use in each situation. Humans sometimes need to learn how to figure things out for themselves, and a good guide makes them aware of how to do it. That means that sometimes I need to back off, get out of their way, and just observe. For me, that balance is like walking a fucking tightrope sometimes. Sometimes I get so frustrated and I want to say, "Can't you see?" But some humans need to walk their paths pretty much alone. Sometimes it's a spiritual lesson for them, and I can't argue with that.

In order to help more than one person at a time, I had to learn how to split or divide myself into a lot of "Eriks." One of my guides taught me how. I call him the Sergeant. It's not his real name; it's just my nickname for him. I call him that because he really makes me stick to my commitment to learn to do things well. I decided that I need to be able to control my splitting when I found out that I had three people thinking about me at the same time, then four, twenty, a hundred . . . and I wanted to be with all of them.

Splitting feels like a natural instinct. I can feel this division happening on its own. It doesn't feel like I'm pulling myself into individual pieces, though. It feels like I'm multitasking in my head, like I can read, write, chew gum, and problem solve but with complete clarity for each of those tasks. I let it all take place on its own, but then I get scared or excited when all these clear thoughts are happening at once. Then the splitting stops. So the Sarge helped me use my heart consciousness to concentrate on being a bunch of Eriks at one time without getting distracted or overstimulated and then crapping out when I want to split into another Erik. How do I explain that if I'm in a hundred places at once and can, with great clarity, understand, feel, work, and give myself to a hundred people at one time, and then I want to do it for a hundred and one? If I'm adding that extra one, it doesn't kill the other hundred just because I'm having that new experience with this new person. He showed me, when I want to split myself some more, how to maintain my focus so I don't get overwhelmed. Actually, it's not a focus, really. It's more like a "let go" feeling. He's like, "Let it happen. Let go." And then it just does.

Splitting into infinite selves feels amazing. Imagine looking at yourself in a mirror and there's another mirror behind you. You see infinite reflections of yourself in the mirror you're facing. My home base is between that first set of facing mirrors, but it doesn't feel like all my other reflected selves are in a different location.

Say I divide into four Eriks so I can help four people on Earth at the same time. I get this sense in each of those four parts of me that what I'm learning and understanding and doing is in reflection number one. At the same time, I'm directly experiencing in reflections two, three, and four. That's because the experiences of all the divided "me's" go back to the home base. But home base is not two miles from Erik one, a hundred miles from Erik two, five feet from Erik three, and six inches from Erik four. Home base is also in each of those four Eriks. It's in every reflection. Does that make sense?

Let me use another analogy. Take a prism. The sunlight that goes through it is my energy, my soul. The prism is the tool I use to divide the sunlight into all the colors of the rainbow, but there's still only one prism and the separate colors still represent the entirety of my light.

Here's another analogy: I take my heart conscious energy and shake it loose like a saltshaker so that all the salt granules are dispersed. This way, I can go to the homes of those blog members, one salt granule at a time. Each granule has my ability to communicate, prank, get information, learn, teach, help, heal, observe, visit my family, and everything else I do—all at the same time. Then when I bring each salt granule back into the saltshaker, it all becomes a part of me again. To someone on Earth, that might seem impossible, but you have to remember that both time and energy work and move differently here.

My main job is being a guide, but I also have other roles. One thing I like to do is help other new spirits communicate with their family members and friends on Earth. Not all spirits have an easy time communicating. Like all the skills we have here, some are better at them than others. So I take the newbie spirit who just died and harass him a little bit. Then I show him the ropes, and after that, I teach him how to pull pranks, give signs, visit his humans through dreams, and communicate in other ways. Eventually I kind of set him free to develop those skills on his own. I don't do that with a lot of random spirits who cross over, though. I usually only help the deceased loved ones of blog members because we already have a connection, but if a blog member dies, I teach him how to connect with family and friends too.

I've also helped people cross over, but I don't do that very often. I've pulled them out of their bodies, told them what's up, handed them off to their wives, children, other spirit guides, whoever. It's an incredible experience, but it's not my expertise. I'll do it especially when a blog member says, "Help, man! Just come and be with my family member while he's dying." Hell yeah, I'll be there. I'll help them with their transition, show them around, and help them get oriented. Another role I have is to help heal people's energy. I didn't know much about it at first. I thought it was like putting a Band-Aid on someone's boo-boo. What I see now is that I help people heal themselves. They have that power, and they've had it all along.

I also help people who want to take their lives, especially those with mental illnesses. If they've tried everything they can—therapy, medicine, whatever—and they're doing their best but are still suffering, I help them with their decision. Society judges people who take their own lives even when it's their time and they're suffering. I'm trying to change that kind of thinking. If it's not a person's time, I guide them to find other ways to get help, and I show them that there's light at the end of the tunnel.

I've saved two lives since I started my job as a guide. The first one was this lady who'd lost her son, just like my mom did. Of course she was a mess. She was going to a therapist once a week, but after four months, she didn't feel any better. I'm not saying therapy is bad. It works for a lot of people. It just wasn't working for her. Anyway, she came home from her last session determined to kill herself. She got everything ready, but all of a sudden she felt this pull to go to her computer and type in, "My son is dead." When she did that, the *Channeling Erik* blog popped up. She read it from the very beginning and wrote in the comments section that she knows that life is worth living.

The second person was this dude who reads the blog all the time but thinks a lot about suicide. He was really unhappy with his life and his relationships, but one particular post changed everything for him. He wrote in the comments section, "I was planning to kill myself today, but after reading this, I want to live." All this makes me feel so good, and I want to help more lives if I can. I *know* I can. It's my job.

Another thing I like to focus on is helping humans understand that there's more to life than what they're experiencing now. Maybe some-one needs to learn how to laugh. Maybe someone needs help receiving communication from spirits. Maybe someone needs help moving for-ward past an obstacle in life. Some just need to see that the best things in life, like building new relationships, are free. Conversation is free. Honesty is free. Vulnerability is free. Loyalty is free. Love is free.

In a nutshell, I help people who are suffering from some kind of loss, someone who feels like they are "without." The loss could be the death of a loved one, the loss of self-esteem, and a hell of a lot of other things. Think of a rubber band. It represents a person's energy. For people who've suffered a loss, their rubber band has been stretched a whole lot, and when something bumps into it, it vibrates. Trauma, loss, or another separation of some kind not only vibrates the rubber band but it also frays it a little bit. That makes it hard for the rubber band to stay taut and keep shit together. So I come in and help pull the pieces back together so that the rubber band can heal itself. How do I do that? I make people become aware of why they feel the way they do and help them feel like they're supported.

This one blog member is a good example. For his entire life, he's always wondered what it was he was searching for. In the simplest terms, he was trying to figure out what a family feels like. For him, even though he loves them, his family didn't feel like what he thought it should. He didn't feel like he had the intimate connections most families have. So I helped him become aware of the different kinds of connections he didn't realize were there. He taught *me* something too. He taught me what patience really means, because, man, that dude was so fucking stubborn. It was worth all the work, though, and I'm grateful to him.

In every case, I help people get moving again. It's all about moving, physically and emotionally. Everyone is different, but the way I help most people mend that frayed part of the rubber band is by bringing things into their life. Here's an example: Say there's this person who really loved nature as a child, but as he got older and started working, raising a family, or experiencing a lot of trauma, he moved away from his connection to nature. What I'd do is get him to look up, notice the sky again, and see how beautiful it looks. That might inspire him to spend more time outdoors like he used to. Or say a person used to love playing a sport when she was in her teens or twenties but she had an injury that prevented her from playing again. I'll bring in things that will help her reestablish that connection to sports, like put her in a place where she meets someone who eventually leads her to an opportunity for a coaching job. It's all about me helping people make connections with things they enjoy, things they need, things they're missing, whatever. Humans are meant to make connections, and connections are what make them move forward.

Actually, moving forward implies a linear movement. It's really more about momentum. In this case, it's a 360-degree expansion or evolution. Momentum can go in any direction. It's not just forward, backward, up, or down. Momentum can move in every direction at once. Take the guy who missed his connection to nature. The first step is reconnecting when he goes outside and enjoys it. That creates a "Wow, this makes me feel good" reaction, and that reaction is another kind of momentum. So are the things he hears or touches or sees. The things this guy is experiencing aren't linear. The moment is happening at the same time and nurturing him from all directions. Maybe he's sitting on a park bench looking at a bird and someone walks over and sits beside him. They might start talking about how much they like birds and decide to join a bird watching club together or maybe just get coffee together and become friends. So then this other person starts having thoughts, emotions, and reactions that radiate outward in all directions and might use this new experience to create more connections. My point is that these connections can go on and on forever, making this huge web. Only one stone thrown in a pond can create ripples across all of it. That stone is a metaphor for a choice to connect. It doesn't take a thousand stones to make all those ripples. It just takes one.

25

Working with Spirit Translators

....

A couple of months after I died, my mom created this blog called *Channeling Erik* to share her experiences processing my death and then my reappearance in her life as a spirit. When it was up and running, I realized that I wanted to communicate with her more like the way we did when I was "alive Erik," so I nudged her to find a spirit translator (or what is popularly known as a medium). I had pretty strict requirements, though. I needed one who doesn't filter me so that all of me can shine through. I needed one who doesn't just say things like, "He's showing me a rose. Does that have any significance for you?" That kind of stuff feels more fortune teller than translator to me. I didn't want my mom to come away thinking, "Oh, they're just making all this up." The perfect spirit translator is one who can describe my personality while translating my thoughts and words—how I look, how I act, what gestures I make, and things like that. That's what really drives it home for my mom. That's where she gets the validation she's looking for.

Anyway, I was lucky enough to find a spirit translator who fits all those qualifications. Her name is Jamie Butler. Like all spirits who get channeled, the spirit translator is like the light a moth is attracted to. I don't want to say that their light is brighter than other people's, because that's not really it; it's just a different kind of light. In Jamie's case, I felt this pull to her. I wouldn't have felt that pull if I didn't have a purpose, but I do. I wanted to talk to my mom so I could help her, and that's when I started to feel Jamie's energy calling to me.

I remember the first time I met Jamie. When my mom had her first channeling session, Jamie hid in a bedroom because she had to be in a place where she wouldn't be interrupted. At first I thought that was pretty weird and not very professional. Then she started to repeat every word I said, and she stumbled on words she didn't want to repeat, like my curse words. She doesn't like dropping f-bombs like I do. She also had a hard time talking to my mom about how I had died. She was afraid it would only worsen her grief. I liked that first session because Jamie's fun to fuck with, but in a good-natured way, and it was a lot of fun watching her cringe and squirm when she had to repeat my bad words. That just made me want to say them more. (Hey, I said I was a spirit guide, but I never said I was mature!) Anyway, over the hour, we became more comfortable with each other. You know how it feels to get out of a cold shower and then wrap yourself in a warm, cozy bathrobe? It was like that.

After that first session, I hung out with Jamie for a little bit and told her everything would be okay. She's so sensitive when young people die, so it was hard for her. She doesn't want anyone, especially mothers, to experience pain—not like that. I thought it went really well, so I pushed my mom to do it again and again. It opened up so many fucking doors between the two of us. Now I have a whole new perspective on communicating between the dimensions. Before that, I was communicating the best way I could through my pranks, signs, and dream visits, but now things are so much better. It brings a whole new side to the way I communicate, and it's wonderful.

A lot of other spirits tell me about their experiences of talking through spirit translators, and the way they describe it is totally different from what happens between Jamie and me. She reacts to me like I'm in the same room with her, which I am. She sees me as a person instead of a memory or idea of a dead dude. Sometimes she gestures with her hands for me to calm down and talk slowly when I give her too much at once. A lot of spirit translators will listen to a spirit and then pause and describe what the spirit said, but Jamie is trained to translate what a spirit says word for word, one after the other right after they're spoken, so she feels me and sees me and hears what I say all at the same time.

Jamie will trance channel me from time to time, and it's both kind of freaky and phenomenal at the same time. Trance channeling is where a spirit takes over a human body and sort of uses it as a puppet. I recognized from her energy pattern that she was open to it. Getting into Jamie's body the first time wasn't that hard. I had to have a little help from her grandfather's spirit, though. He showed me how to change her energy pattern to enter her body through the side of her neck. That's the easiest place to get in. He also gave me the rules and regulations. He told me that it's important to know what kind of shape her body is in and to pay attention to that, like if she has a cold or an itchy rash. That's because Jamie has this rule that the spirits she trance channels have to help heal her body while they're in it. Since she shares space with them, she wants them to leave her body in better shape than when they were in it.

When I stand next to Jamie, I can see the way her soul moves out of her body. It's kind of like this cocoon of white light that moves out of her upper back, neck, and head. I don't really know where the hell she goes or what she does when she's gone, though. Anyway, as she leaves, I center myself and stand right next to her to go in, and then I just focus my heart consciousness on what I'm about to do.

Once I'm in her body, I mimic her human actions and communication. At first, it was a little awkward because I'd forgotten all the physical things I'd felt when I was a human. I'd forgotten how to take a breath, the feel of hair on my scalp, the feel of clothes against my skin, the feel of *any* skin at all.

I feel emotional reactions too. As a free spirit, I have these amazing emotions that don't come with physical reactions. When I get excited, I don't sweat, my heart doesn't start racing, and I don't lose my breath. I don't cry when I'm happy either. These things just don't happen in an energetic body, but when I'm inside Jamie's body and her heart is beating fast, her palms are sweaty, and her emotions are really thick, I feel all those things firsthand too. After a while, I started to feel comfortable with it, though, and I began to remember what it was like to have a human body. When I look out through Jamie's eyes, I can still see everybody, but I can also see their energy. I guess it's like how she sees people. She sees their auras, and she has to work really hard to look beyond them to see their physical body.

One of the first things I remember about being inside Jamie was her mousy little voice. I guess I would have preferred a deeper voice that was more like mine when I was alive. Think about it: I spent all those years focused on being a dude who loves being, well, a *dude*, and here I was in this short little chick with boobs and a high voice. It was bizarre. But ultimately the physical body didn't matter. I was just happy to be in it because, by that time, I had been working with Jamie for so long that it was like being in a vacation home where you know all the nooks and crannies.

My first experience with trance channeling was during an event Jamie put on for blog members called "The *Channeling Erik* Weekend of F-ing Enlightenment." As I'm sure you can tell by the f-bomb, the name was my idea. My mom was in the audience, but I remember she wasn't in the front row. She was hiding in the back, and I had to get up and run to her. I wanted to hug my mom, so I moved Jamie's arms and threw them around her. The arms moved, but they didn't go through her. They stopped on the surface of her body, and I wasn't used to that. When I hugged her, she felt so little. I liked feeling her touch and smelling her hair like I did when I was alive. I just wanted to savor it. It had been a long time.

The moment we held each other seemed like the end of a race. It was like crossing a finish line at the end of a marathon you'd just run without shoes on—there was a lot of pain but a lot of relief too. In that moment, I think we both processed a lot of stuff that had been hard for us to come to terms with. It was hard to look back on the things my mom and I had been through. It was hard because of the contract my soul had made for my life as Erik in which I had to suffer so much. It was hard because I'd taken my life—something society doesn't accept. It was hard because I was a young man when I died, and that's really sad. It was hard because of the messy way I'd taken my life. It was hard because I'd left a family behind and because they didn't yet have a spiritual understanding of where I'd gone. That stuff started to change when we met Jamie, though.

I've grown to love Jamie a lot. We have this very intimate relationship. I don't mean a romantic one, because that'd be weird. I just feel like she's my sister. I think she's really nice, but sometimes she's too nice. She needs to learn how to fucking say no. She's also humble and underestimates her abilities, but I do admire that whatever she does, whether it's building a shed or taking care of her kids or doing her work, she always wants to do her best. I like that she's emotionally honest too. Humans like that are hard to find.

Jamie and I have gotten to know each other well. She's comfortable with me now—comfortable enough that I can push her buttons all the time. I love doing that. She's usually a good sport about it, but sometimes she puts her foot down and fusses at me for crossing her boundaries. I get on her nerves sometimes. It's like she's this annoyed big sister scolding her pesky little brother. I also find some of the things Jamie does endearing, like her funny gestures, some of her hang-ups, and stuff like that. Sometimes I feel like I need to protect her, though, because a lot of times she takes on too much and it stresses her out, but she's so independent, so a lot of the time she thinks, "It's my lesson, so I need to do it on my own."

I know I've already said this, but I'm so thankful that Jamie entered our lives when she did. I think it was perfect timing, and I'm glad that I'm one of the spirits lucky enough to have formed a lasting relationship with a spirit translator like Jamie. Some people are always gonna think that translators are frauds or are only in it for the money and to exploit people or whatever, and I've got two things to say to that: One, everyone's entitled to their own thoughts and opinions. The second—and final—thing I have to say to the people who doubt or judge my mom or Jamie is this: Don't spend your energy on judgment! It's never worth it. I suggest you direct that energy back on yourself and the health of your own soul and the souls around you. That's what it's all about.

26

The Blog

....

So yeah, my mom has this blog called *Channeling Erik*. She needed to vent her grief, and she felt like she could do that best by reaching out to a community that needed to do the same. The blog also helps her continue to explore ways to heal. The need to heal was a soul contract that she carried into this life at birth, a contract her soul had designed for itself.

Even though the blog grew directly from her pain, it's grown into something so much more than that. And even though it started out as a way for her to address her own needs, it fed everything I needed too. I wasn't asking that of her, and I wasn't encouraging her to do it. Eventually, it proved to be something that maybe I wanted even more than she did. Part of my purpose as a guide is to reach a lot of people, so I have to have some sort of platform for that to happen. Since it came from within her, the blog's her baby, but it also gives me a place to do my thing, so I guess I can call it my baby too.

My mom had everything in place to do something like this. She had already published books. They're about parenting, and I probably gave her a lot of material for them. Raising five kids kind of makes her an expert. She's already respected in her community as a doctor too, so that also helps. I'm glad she chose to create the blog because it's something that gives me the voice I need to help people in really practical ways. I guess if she didn't make any sort of soapbox for me, I would have found other ways to help people on Earth, and I still would have communicated with my family. Still, it's nice to have this working relationship together.

I love every single one of the blog members. I love haunting them; I love helping them; I love when they first stumble across the blog and they don't even realize how they got there in the first place. I also like it when they get to the part where they understand that I can be a little bit of a dick and that I like to harass people sometimes. I think it's funny as fuck. Humor's important, even—sometimes especially—when you're a spirit. Even if we never post anything from this day forward, the blog's going to live on the internet forever and people will find it. When they do, I hope it will continue to be the answer some people are seeking.

27

Making Myself Heard

....

The first time I was interviewed on the radio was through Jamie. I wasn't nervous or anything. I was just really excited. It's weird because at first I could feel what everyone was feeling and thinking— the host, the listeners, everybody. I was connected to their energy. In the beginning, I had trouble filtering all that "noise" out, but now I can focus on just the questions and my answers.

I like radio shows and YouTube videos because it's incredible to have a voice for a large number of people. Since the publication of my mom's book *My Son and the Afterlife*, lots of people want to hear our story on TV or the radio. During one of the first radio shows she was interviewed on, I made myself heard. No one heard me during the live interview. The host picked up on it when she listened to the recording, though. You might ask, "Why can't we hear it when it's happening?" Well, why can't humans hear dog whistles? They can't detect that frequency with their ears, but digital recording equipment can. It's more sensitive than the human ear. It's pretty easy because the energy is already flowing. It's like I stick my finger in a water current and it bends around it; so I stick my pattern of energy into the other sounds in the interview.

I've also left my voice on some of the YouTube videos my mom makes with Jamie. One time a blog member was watching one of those videos and contacted my mom to tell her she heard voices on it. Well, one of those voices belonged to yours truly. Just like voices on the radio show, it could only be heard on the playback. No one heard it when it was being recorded. My mom was pretty intrigued, so she got some sound guru to analyze it. The guy was puzzled because my voice didn't leave a voiceprint like it would with human voices. Well, guess what: I don't have vocal cords! I know you might think that sound is sound, but it's not the same pattern. Spirits' voices have more range and more energy, and we can include thought energy that the machines can't pick up.

EVP stands for electronic voice phenomena, and it's a great way for spirits to communicate with the loved ones we leave behind. When I heard that spirits could leave their voices on recorders, I decided I wanted to learn how. There's this human dude in Italy who runs an EVP center. He has a lot of electronic devices that can pick up EVPs really well, and tons of spirits go there to observe the really badass spirits who are good at communicating through electrical devices. These spirits help us change our energetic makeup so that it flows along the sound waves and electrical patterns to leave the voice imprint. There are many of these centers around the world where we can do this, but the guy in Italy is really good. How do I do it? I just interact with the electrical energy to leave an imprint of my voice. It's kind of like a dance, and the dance leaves an impression. It's like leaving a fingerprint on a glass but it's a digital imprint, not a voice one.

When I'm leaving an EVP, most of the time the person's recording but not listening to me talking at that time. Then they stop and rewind it, push play, and hear themselves asking questions like, "Is there anyone here with me?" Then they'll hear my voice, "Yeah, it's me, Erik."

Again, think of it like a dog whistle. It's a frequency the human ear can't pick up but the recorder can. It's easier because we don't have to lower our frequency to make it louder for the human ear. The digital recorder does that for me. I'd be the first one to promote using EVPs to communicate with your loved ones, especially if you're having a hard time with other methods.

I've also learned a lot of about how to give signs and pranks to other humans like the blog members by mimicking what other spirits do. Now that the blog has grown so much, I'm diving in deeper because I want to know all I can about helping more people. I'm trying to learn more with the help of Cawli and other guides, my family members here, and my close circle of spirit friends. I pull pranks and give signs to blog members for a different reason than when I do it with my family. This is how I reach out to them as a guide. It's how I get them roped in so I can reach them, but, of course, I also do it because I like seeing them freak out. They like when I prank them, too, because it makes them feel special. I don't do anything to scare them, though; like I would never put my face a few inches from theirs while they're sleeping and then shout, "Boo!" the minute they open their eyes.

One time I made a specific song air on the radio for a blog member. She loved it, and she knew it was from me. Usually, the person I want to send the message to has this subconscious intention. Deep inside, they want to hear that special song. That intention is energy, and it sort of melds with my energy to help make it happen. I love water analogies, so I'll use one to explain it: A person sends out ripples in a pond, and those ripples represent a certain song they want to hear. I'm on the other side of the pond, going, "Ah, I see your ripples. I'm gonna send some back." So I send ripples back, and when the ripples collide, the song plays.

Sometimes, when I give really tangible signs, I get so fucking irritated when I don't get the response I want. I work so hard to light a candle or flip a switch, but still some people stop and think, "Well, that was nice, but I want to know if it was really you. I need more." That's why I like to play pranks that fit the "Erik" personality they're familiar with. Then they're more likely to know, without a doubt, that it's me.

I realize that I'm kind of a little shit a lot of the time when I communicate, but that's just my style. Some spirits communicate with a calming presence 100 percent of the time, and others communicate with more of an energized, motivational style. Me? This is just how I'm made, and if I tried to communicate differently, I don't think I'd be able to reach nearly as many people or do my job as well. You know how your parents and your teachers and stuff are always telling you, "Be yourself!" when you're growing up? Well, it's true for spirits too. We have to be ourselves—who and how we are doesn't always resonate with everyone, but that's okay. Even if I just change a handful of lives for the better by being who I am and not compromising, then I'll still be doing my job.

28

Having Fans

....

I have my fair share of fans, and I love 'em. Shit yeah. I wish I'd had more of them when I was alive because then I would have had more true friends—and let's be honest, I probably would have gotten laid more, which would have been awesome. Now the compliments are really nice, but not in the way that they boost my ego like they would have when I was a human. I don't have an ego anymore— no spirit really does. I see that the compliments are not about me; I don't need them, but they do, and that's the important part. But I still appreciate them. I feel and process everybody's emotions toward me, so when it's sweet and loving and flattering, I feel it all over. And when I'm fed all of this loving energy, it makes my energy even more powerful and expansive. That makes it easier for me to use all of my abilities as a guide.

Some people get too emotionally connected to me. They get enthralled by me so much that they stop focusing on their life and don't use the information I'm trying to give them; instead, they just use the information for entertainment. It's a challenge for me to guide them back to listening to the message itself and go back to focusing on their lives, but it's worth the hard work.

I don't think it's bad that some people get a little obsessed with the concept of me sometimes, because that's a very a human thing. It's like, people often think things like, "That person's cool," or "That person's got something I would like to know or have," so they use that person as a model. It's just a style of growth that some humans go through, so I think it's totally okay, but it goes over the top, like they hand me all their shit and say, "Erik, you're my hero. You gotta do this for me. You gotta fix this for me." I'll be the first to step in and go, "Um, what?" I'll listen, and I'll help, but they have to do the work too. I'm not Mr. Fix It. I'm Mr. I'll Fix It With You.

29

Making Believers
Out of the Human Race

······································

I really, really want people to believe that I'm still alive in some other dimension and that all this shit is real. The person I most wanted to believe this was my mom. Before I died, she didn't really believe that there was a life after death, but after I died, I knew she had to believe. Her journey from skepticism to belief is part of her soul's contract, but it's also been about survival for her. I couldn't just go, "Eh, I'm just going to sit around here; she'll figure it out on her own." That'd be such a dick move! The thing is, I felt all my mom's pain along with her. I still do, and that shit is nearly unbearable. My pain and hers is a hell of an incentive. So a lot of my motivation has been to help her understand grief and to help her see that what's at the end of her nose isn't all there is.

My mom was someone who, for a long time, believed only in the things she sees with her eyes, smells with her nose, tastes with her tongue, hears with her ears, or touches with her fingers. There has to be a scientific explanation behind it. Well, with spiritual things, you can't always have empirical proof—that's just not always how our energy flows in the spiritual dimensions. There are no equations that spit out concrete, tangible answers.

So what I did was take what she does believe in and use that to my advantage. Since she believes in sight, I moved shit and did other things she could see, like show up as a moving ball of light called an orb in a photograph Michelle took just a few days after I died. That's one of the first things that gave my mom hope. I also messed with her other senses by pranking her. I needed to show her that there's an outside me away from the one inside her head that science or psychiatry might dismiss as imagination. Of course, she had to be willing to participate in that journey, and I know she was. This is how I wanted to stop the internal bleeding that grief causes and help her move on and grow, and, in turn, help others.

The first time I appeared to my mom as my human-form self after I died was when she was lying in her bed a while after I'd passed. Before she even closed her eyes, she saw me hopping at the foot of her bed. When her eyes met mine, I was shocked, and I could tell she was too. I wasn't even trying to get her to see me, I was just fucking around. Shit, I'm around her all the time and she'd never seen me before, so it was the last thing I expected to happen. I realized later that it was because her energy had finally opened up to me and pulled me in. It wasn't just a one-way street anymore; our energies were going in both directions, and then—*poof!*—there I was, right before her eyes.

Usually when I manifest on purpose like I did with Poppi back in those first days as a spirit, I pull in all my heart-centered consciousness to get this sharp focus on my intention to make it happen. Since my energy doesn't really resonate naturally with material things, I have to get the whole core of my energetic body and use it to slow down my vibrational frequency. Pretend like I'm a blender on a really high speed. You look in the blender and all you see is a big blur, but with the power of thought and love and heart-centered consciousness, I can slow the blender down so it doesn't mix things up so fast. That makes it easier to see what's in the blender. Then I have to figure out how that person, like Poppi, is going to acknowledge me the easiest. I have to consider and focus on both the environment I'm in and the person I'm trying to reach. I can't just knock on their door and, when they open it, shout, "Ta-da!" There are more variables than just concentrating on myself.

When my mom first saw me after I'd died, she was the one who pulled me in. She needed to see me so bad, and I was ready to reveal myself to her, and at the same time, she's also finally reached a certain level of calmness and openness that made her tune right in to my frequency. Usually when I'm in my house on the earthly plane where my energy frequency is higher than my mom's, she can't see me. My energy vibrates at a level above where humans can see things, but because her state of mind was the way it was for so long after I died, we could only meet each other halfway. It's fucking hard for spirits to slow down enough to reach people who are grieving because they vibrate at the bottom of the visible part of the energy spectrum. This is why people use terms like, "I'm depressed," "I'm feeling low," or "I'm feeling down."

The difference between what happened when I first really appeared to my mom and what happened when I appeared in front of Poppi was that I wasn't knocking on my mom's door, because I knew that she wasn't yet ready to open it. I knocked on his, and I changed myself in a way that he could understand because he wasn't grieving a lot. We really didn't know each other that much, and he didn't care about me as much as my mom and the rest of my family did. No dig at Poppi here; it's just a simple fact. Anyway, I changed my looks, my age, and the way I talked to him so he could see me the way he would recognize me. With my mom, I didn't have to do that. I just had to be me and wait around until she woke the fuck up. I mean, when her consciousness woke, not when she woke up from a dream. It's so much easier for me to manifest physically when someone like her pulls on my energy compared to when I have to do it without a person's participation. Other than the call from Poppi letting her know that he'd seen me and my appearing in that photo as an orb of light, this visit was the first one that gave her hope.

A few earthly months after that, I was feeling more creative than usual, and I wanted to get her attention. I wanted her to be okay, and things were not okay for her that day. Electrical currents are easy for me to fuck with because I'm kind of like an energy current myself, so I can mix my energy with the electrical energy of the current that goes to a telephone and manipulate it. Also, I didn't have to go through the whole telephone system. It's not like, "You know, I want to call my mom, so I'm going to manifest myself over in Virginia where the relay station is and dial her number." I can go straight to the house and mess with the instrument itself. I didn't consciously fuck with the answering machine part of it, so I didn't leave a message. I just consciously screwed around with the telephone part, so when the machine picked up, I said, "Mom, it's me, Erik. It's me." She flew to the phone. She didn't pick it up in time, but she knew it was me because she's a mom, and moms know the sound of their own kid's voice. It kind of freaked her out that the caller ID showed a twelve-digit number, and when she tried to call it, it wasn't a working line. She also looked at the message count, and it read, "0." She didn't understand how she could have heard my voice without it being picked up by the answering machine. I wish I had left a recording back then. I could have, but I didn't. I was just focused on getting her attention. Still, it made her happy.

I've pranked other family members too. It's the only way I know how to get their attention and get them to smile. It's my way of communicating and connecting with them. I think that if I were more of a ho-hum kind of guy, like a straight shooter, I'd go up and say, "Well, hi, Michelle. How are you?" That's not what I want to do. I like pranks that they won't be able to dismiss or forget. That's why I give them pranks and signs that are in-your-face. I've heard that a lot of other spirits have wonderful communications with a person when they enter their dreams, but I don't like that as much because that person can totally write it off later on and think, "That was really my imagination. It really didn't happen."

The main reason I like to prank my family and stuff is because it's fucking fun! Of course, I also do it to comfort them. It helps them know that I'm not gone forever, and it's a way of expressing my personality in a way that they recognize. One of my favorite pranks for my family is working with electronics, like turning TVs, appliances, or computers off and on, calling them on the phone like I did with my mom, making a specific song play on the radio like I mentioned I do with blog members, or shuffling their playlists so that a certain song comes on. I try to make it so that the songs always have meaning for them, like a special message. I do all these things by restructuring energy. Like I said earlier, electricity is a really easy energy to screw with because it's most similar to our energetic bodies. It's not like this "If I touch it, then I'm going to be shocked" thing, so I'm not afraid of the electrical current. I just manifest a certain kind of energy, put it into the existing electrical current, and then manipulate the polarity to block the current or change the direction of its flow. TVs, radios, iPods, blenders, computers, telephones, and others are already programmed to do the shit they do, so I don't have to create a new program. I just rewrite how the current or wave is being processed in the wire.

One of the first times I worked with an appliance was when I wanted to get Pappa's attention. Several times when he came home from work and walked through the door that leads into the kitchen, I'd make the downdraft vent—the kind that pops up from the counter to suck up smells and smoke from stuff cooking on the stove—go up and down. It's like I was saying "Hi" to him. The thing is, not only was it unplugged but they were remodeling the kitchen at the time, so there was no power in the room—and I mean *no* power. I thought it was really funny to see the electrician scratch his head trying to figure what the fuck was going on.

I can also actually move things. It's not that easy for me. It's not like how you can take your finger, push on a Coke can, and make it slide across a counter. I have to lower the frequency of a spot around the can and push that energy forward with my energy. The energy is the one I mentioned that comes in through the jellyfish filter. I just lower the frequency of that energy to make it denser so that it matches the frequency of matter on the earthly plane. When I do that, it's like something dense moving another thing that's at least as dense. You can't move a Coke can easily by blowing on it because the density of air is not high enough to move something heavy. It's similar to the way I moved things when I was alive, so it's kind of like touch.

Once when my mom and a couple of her friends were eating at some Mexican restaurant, I made the salt and pepper shakers slide off the table. At first, they thought the waiter's apron might have caught on them, so they moved the shakers to the center of the table. No big deal. I made them slide off the table two more times.

I've moved other things too. One time when my sister Michelle was in my mom's bathroom raiding her makeup drawer, I made the sink faucet slowly turn on almost all the way. Man, you should have heard that scream. I've also turned a deadbolt to lock my family in the kitchen so they couldn't get to the car and drive somewhere to eat lunch. They laughed because they all knew it was me.

It's easier to move stuff if I have another person's energy to play off of, a person I have a bond with. Once I spun the water bottle around on the nightstand next to my niece, Arleen's, bed by pulling in her welcoming energy. I guess the process kind of magnifies the energy and creates this resistance that gets the two energies to repel each other. It kind of works like when the negative pole of one magnet pushes the other magnet's negative pole to make them move away from each other. The resistance pushing one side of the bottle made it spin.

Soon after my death, I decided to cheer up my sister Kristina. She was a medical student at the time, so she didn't really have a chance to put her studies aside and grieve. One evening when she had her nose in her books, I put my plan into action. She had this little altar set up on the desk that had a lit candle on it. I started making the flame wiggle, and that startled her. The air conditioner was off and there were no windows open, so she couldn't figure out how the flame could move. She looked at the candle and said, "Get tall." I made it stretch upward. Then she said, "Get small," so I made it shrink. The commands continued: "Dance," "Stay still," and then she said, "Move to the left." That's when things got a little creepy to her because I made the flame move half an inch over so that it totally disconnected from the wick.

I learned how to drop things from the ceiling, too, like when I dropped an airsoft BB right in front of my mom. All I had to do was create the BB with my thoughts and then lower its vibrational frequency to match the frequency of matter on the earthly plane. When that frequency dropped into the visible range of the energy spectrum, my mom could see it. It made her happy because she knew it was me. I used to play war with airsoft guns with my brother, sisters, and some of the kids from the neighborhood, so it brought back good memories for her.

Entering a person's dream is sort of like surfing. I've done that a lot of times with my sister Michelle. It's hard to explain how it works, but here's what it's not: it's not like a person is lying down having a dream and the dream shows up in this little bubble hovering above them with a line drawn to their head and I just jump in. When people are in a dream state, their brain waves are in a certain pattern that represents where their consciousness is. Their consciousness kind of projects itself into a different dimension that's closer to mine. That's because the frequency of the dream state is pretty close to the frequency of the spiritual realm. So let's say a person's dreaming in the fifth dimension and I'm vibrating in the sixth one. It's easy for me to find that space where they're doing their dream manifestation and invite myself in. It's not like I can just hop into *everyone's* dreams, though. I make sure that the experience is what they need, so I only enter the dreams of people I know I can help.

Hiding an object is really fun, and I do it lots of different ways. I can interfere with the person's vision so that they can't see it. That's just when I want to hide something from that one person. If I want to hide something from everyone, I manipulate the energy in front of the object so that it mirrors the space behind, making it look invisible. It's like an invisibility cloak. I can also do it by dismantling that object's energy and then reassembling it in another location. Think like, "Beam me up, Scotty." One time, I hid my mom's to-do list. She writes it on index cards. Because she's a little obsessive about that sort of thing, she panicked, but I made it reappear so that it stuck out of the purse she'd searched a million times. That kind of thing drives my whole family crazy, but it's all done out of love.

I love making my family feel goose bumps. It's kind of the main way I try to communicate with my mom, and it's different from the regular goose bumps a person might feel. It's more intense, and I try to focus it on just one part of their body so they feel like they're being touched or hugged. I can create the sensation one of two ways. First, I can alter the air or the energy next to the person's skin by merging the outer layer of my energetic field with theirs. I have to lower the frequency of my energy so they can feel it, though. It needs to be a close match to their frequency, like I said before. It's kind of like moving objects where I need something that's close to solid to move a solid. Another way I can do it is by screwing with the spot in their brain that creates the goose-bumps sensation. I just hit that button.

Making smells is kind of my specialty, and they're never like roses or perfume. I like to create the really nasty ones, like cigar smoke, rotten fish, pot, farts, smelly socks, and other rank smells. All I have to do is figure out the energy signature of that smell on Earth and duplicate it. That's pretty easy. It's like reading a recipe from a cookbook and cooking it. Then I get right next to the person I want to annoy and I put that same smelly energy pattern copy in their space. I find it hilarious when they wrinkle up their noses and cough, especially when there's not a dog around to blame.

A lot of humans get visits from birds, butterflies, and other insects after a family member or friend dies, and they think their loved one all of a sudden, like, turned into a bug or a bird something. I can see how someone would think that, but it's not quite true. It's a special moment for them, though, so I use my energy to steer anything that can fly. I usually use dragonflies because they're pretty easy to steer. All I have to do is use my energy to manipulate the energy around the dragonfly so it can fly in the direction I want it to go. It's kind of like flying a drone. The energy around the insect feeds into the energy of the insect, so I start there and go in. I've done this to my mom lots of times. Once I made a dragonfly go around her in circles, around and around and around, and then I made it sit still on the chair right next to her. I've done it to my dad too. He races motorcycles, and you know me, I love being around anything with wheels. So one long weekend, when my dad was at the track, I made a big orange dragonfly follow him wherever he went. I even made it sit on his shoulder for a couple of hours. I liked chilling with him for those three days, but it kind of made him freak out a little. Not in a bad way, though. He liked it because he knew it was me. I just made sure not to have it sit on his shoulder when he was racing, because his bike is fast and I don't think the dragonfly would appreciate that very much.

My mom's mom—she likes to be called Big Mama—Aunt Denise, and I like to fly insects around. It's our way of playing together. Big Mama likes to steer monarch butterflies because she thinks they're pretty. Aunt Denise likes to use a tattered moth. I don't have any fucking idea why. I guess I could ask her. Of course, my favorite is dragonflies, but I like to use different colored ones, like orange ones, black ones, and the usual green ones.

The point of screwing around and having fun with people on Earth is to chip away at their skepticism bit by bit. I don't want to do it in scary ways or ways that are too intense all at once—that would be counterproductive. I prefer to let loose, enjoy myself, and try to make these experiences enjoyable for the people whose lives I touch too. After all, what would the point be if I just ended up scaring people off instead of inviting them to open their minds and hearts and explore with me?

30

Relationships

···

My relationship with my mom has changed because we talk more than we ever did when I was "alive." We talk about shit we didn't know how to discuss before. Our love for each other is deeper. Our respect for each other is deeper, and I think what makes this relationship so wonderful is that we don't have to worry about the other one getting hurt. Now I understand that when humans get hurt, there's a greater story to it and shit like that. I get that now, so I don't get all twisted up about things like that, and my mom knows that, shit, I'm not going to die again. We're solid on that front, and her knowing that has really changed our relationship. I want our connection to get even deeper and that'll mean us having our own private conversations without a spirit translator, conversations that are apart from the blog. She does hear me. She channels me, but she doesn't trust herself.

My relationship with the rest of my family is different now. It's deeper, at least from my end. I get to see them—my dad, my siblings, everyone—for exactly who they are and how they feel. They still grieve, and I know that grieving is very difficult, but a lot of time has passed since I did what I did, so I think that time's doing what it does and does well in that respect—healing wounds that you never think are going to heal, but with time, they always do.

As far as my relationship with myself, that's changed too. I can say I love and respect myself without it being egotistical. I love myself. I really do. I just fucking love who I am and how I help, interact, and communicate with other people in a way I never did when I was alive. Now I'm this beautiful light energy. I care for myself. I didn't love or care for myself when I was alive. Back then there were parts of me that I really didn't like and couldn't really relate to, but now I don't have that inner voice that used to fuck with me all the time. When I say I love and care for myself now, it's kind of fucked up because that sounds like there's judgment involved, but there isn't. Now I also see that I'm someone who helps, and I've worked hard to get to where I am now. That makes me proud.

31

Being an Accomplished Guide

....

I'm very proud of the accomplishments I've made since I crossed over, but it's not just the pride that's inside me. It feels broader than that. My pride is located across the world instead of just inside me. I don't look at it and go, "I did *this* today!" or "I said this important thing. Go, me!" It's not like I think I'm hot shit or anything. That's all ego stuff, and like I said, spirits don't really have egos. What I get out of it is the feeling that comes with helping a person, including my mom. Part of the way she heals is by helping others, and what I communicate through the blog lets her do that, and it lets her know that I didn't just disappear. I help a lot of other people with that. I help them be more comfortable with death and what happens afterward. That's a reward in and of itself.

Let me explain it this way: When I help a person's life, not only am I proud of the work I've done but I'm also proud of them for fighting. I'm proud of them for accepting my help and taking it to the point where they turn the corner to save themselves. In every teacher-student relationship, things don't just flow in one direction. It's not just me who knows all and fixes things for them. I can know all and give direction, sure, but they have to follow those directions and make of them what they will. They have to own it. They have to do the work. They have to fight for it. So my pride doesn't stay in me. It's in every single person's path that we've come across, and by "we," I mean my mom and me—our blog, our story, and the books. It's about how people have changed the way they see their lives and how they want to live it. My pride is in them for wanting and making the changes.

The *Channeling Erik* community allows people to explore spirituality together. They might get an awareness of the wonderment that's beyond the life they know. They might come to understand the reasons behind the human experience and become less fearful of death. I think the blog has helped define the spiritual realm with everyday language, and that helps people understand it better.

I've helped stop people from taking their own lives by letting them see that there are people in the same situation they're in. Through the blog, they have a place to talk about it, and that's what people need to feel connected to the world and to other people again. We show them the way back to the value of the human experience. You know, some people feel so separated from everything. It's not their fault, really; that's not how it works. They just feel like they're trapped in a box and can't communicate with others. Connecting is the answer, but you can't connect if you don't have the tools. Our blog helps put those kinds of people in touch with each other. Once they do and have those, "Oh, shit! Me too. Me too!" moments, then they can reconnect to the sweetness in life. That's what the blog does. It connects people who feel like they're alone, and that can change everything.

Another really important thing we do on the blog is to remind people how fucking precious their lives are. Your life on Earth is a choice your soul makes, and when you're actually living it and not getting mired down in all the day-to-day shit that makes life so damn hard sometimes, it's easy to connect with the big picture—that this is the path your soul has chosen to walk. Sometimes the blog helps people figure out why they did something dumb or embarrassing or hurtful and why suffering is sometimes just a way to grow.

I encourage people to ride the roller coaster of life for as long as they can, because it's so special to be alive as a human. The experiences and the beauty and the connections your soul needs to evolve and thrive are all made on Earth, and you carry those with you into the afterlife. Helping educate people about these things makes me feel complete and satisfied as a guide. I'm so invigorated by my work that I don't ever want to stop.

I remember this one time I helped this guy find the purpose in his life and what a gift it was to do so. He was a forty-eight-year-old man. He was one of the first ones I helped on my own without my guides helping me along the way. I think of him as my first solo flight. This dude had been thinking about killing himself for weeks. He even bought a gun—a shotgun. He'd had enough of life for lots of reasons. Life just became too fucking heavy for him. He was suffering too much, and he didn't know how to find relief. It mostly had to do with control. He wanted to control how long a job lasted, how long a relationship lasted, and how certain family members and friends listened to him or didn't. Suicide was the way he chose to express his anger, disappointment, and frustration with everything life had been throwing at him.

One night he was shit-faced drunk, sitting on a couch, thinking this was the day he was going to do it. So he got up, went to his back-yard, and sat on a bench that had a wooden fence behind it. First I started fucking with him a little bit. I don't mean to make light of the situation, but I'd whisper to him, "How are you going to put that shotgun in your face? Think about it. What if you just blow off part of your face? Dude, you're fucking drunk as shit, so your coordination sucks. You're gonna screw this up, and you're probably going to regret it." I was feeding this information to his subconscious energetically. Eventually, he put the shotgun off to the side and thought, *You know, maybe this isn't the best thing*. He kind of stumbled back into his house, washed his face, and then sat in front of his computer. What he didn't realize just then was that washing his face was a metaphor for starting to cleanse some of the shit he'd been holding on to. Then the real magic started. He did a search about death and suicide. He wanted to make sure that there was something afterward waiting for him before he went through with it. He came across the *Channeling Erik* blog and started reading it. While he did this, he started to discover other people's stories and he started to empathize with them and see himself in them. He came to understand that there's a purpose to life. I'm so fucking proud of how he turned himself around. That was super brave.

I've learned so much as a spirit and as a guide, but I think the biggest lessons are my ability to love and my ability to connect emotionally to everything and everyone, including myself. That came from realizing that I'm an emotional being. In other words, I'm energy made from emotion. Humans are also emotional beings, and once they figure that out, then they'll be able to put their emotions—especially empathy and love—first and start to make those same connections.

Another thing that's been really groundbreaking for me is learning that separation is an illusion. I know it sounds like bullshit when you're feeling super lonely and like no one understands what you're going through, and believe me, I get that. But do me a favor: The next time you get that feeling of separation and loneliness, go outside and look up at the stars. Try to remember that, even though it feels like you're alone—especially if you've lost someone you love—you're a part of the fabric of the universe and so are they, and you're both connected to everything that ever was, is, and will be. We're here watching over you, and if you need us, get in touch. Reach out. Join an online community or a support group or just talk to your angels or guides in whatever way that you feel is most authentic. We're here to listen, man. You're not alone.

32

My Thoughts on Humanity

···

It sucks, it sucks, it sucks to watch the human race struggle. If people just had a little more patience with themselves and the world, then they'd be able to see that they create a lot of their own struggles. They don't see all the opportunities that are presented to them through those struggles. You know how there's that old adage "History repeats itself"? Well, that's pretty fucking true. Look at all the wars, the injustices, all that shit we've been dealing with for literally thousands of years. But guess what: if we actually took a step back collectively as a race of beings and made a conscious effort to learn from our past mistakes, then we might actually get somewhere. I think that human beings are doing that, slowly. Progress is being made; it's just slow and hard. But that's just part of the cosmic bargain.

We spirits don't see global issues like the unrest in the Middle East and hunger and disease and stuff like that as a bad thing. That sounds really cold and heartless, but remember, "good" and "bad" don't really exist on the spirit level. It's all part of an ongoing process of evolution. Suffering and conflict make people aware of what they want and don't want. It helps them choose what creates suffering and what alleviates it, what serves them and what doesn't.

As spirits, we kind of watch everything play out on the world stage from the wings, but we're also slowly finding our voice again to bring about a global awareness of human suffering. I think that the way people process suffering is a lesson in global connection, or lack thereof. When this shit comes on TV, half the people don't fucking want to tune in. It's like, "What the fuck. That's a world away. I'm sitting on my couch, and I can't connect to that directly, so I'm just gonna tune out." The other half of the people get angry, and you can't have resolution with anger. There'll be a few people, though, who rise up, like Gandhi or Martin Luther King Jr. or even just a kid who stands up to a schoolyard bully. They'll rise up and just say, "Enough." That's part of the larger dance of learning from pain and injustice too.

People feel like they don't have the power to make change because they feel so small compared to the big problems of the world. They don't feel like they can make things shift in another direction. But, hey, let me tell you, we have the best fucking tool in the universe: the internet. It's about sharing information, and if we could just continue to pull people together and have them communicate more, oh shit, so much good stuff could happen. The internet gives humans the power to get together heart to heart and emotion to emotion and thought to thought across the boundaries of culture, countries, and continents to make the world a better place. As a spirit, sometimes it's frustrating to watch people suffer, but it's also encouraging to watch them learn from that suffering and move forward, and it's really cool to watch how a lot of people are using modern technology to help them do that.

This is why my main focus of helping people out is concerned with the blog. I also get together with groups of spirits that sort of work with people on a subconscious level, especially different world leaders. We try to get them to appreciate life no matter what form it takes, whether it's evolving through suffering or not. We try to teach people to find emotional balance, no matter what their soul's contracts have in store for them. I don't work with these groups much, though. I mostly try to help one person at a time.

Will there still be war, pain, suffering, and things like that as humanity continues to evolve? Yeah. It won't ever be wiped off the face of the Earth. It'll get better as long as people keep learning from their mistakes and keep trying to love each other before hating each other, but it won't go away completely because pain can teach us just as much as happiness. I really do think it all comes down to empathy, though. If you recognize pain in someone, try to reach out and understand his or her experience, and if you're experiencing pain, try to reach out for help. I know I've said I'm not a big reader, and that's true for sure, but there's this one thing that the author Kurt Vonnegut said that I think pretty much nails it on the fucking head. It goes like this:

> "Hello, babies. Welcome to Earth. It's hot in the summer and cold in the winter. It's round and wet and crowded. On the outside, babies, you've got a hundred years here. There's only one rule that I know of, babies—'God damn it, you've got to be kind.'"*

---

*Kurt Vonnegut, *God Bless You, Mr. Rosewater, or Pearls Before Swine* (Boston: Holt, Rinehart and Winston, 1965), 129.

Closing Thoughts

....

I've gotten so much out of this entire experience since my death. I got myself. Even though time doesn't move in a linear fashion here like it does on Earth, if I were to look at my path as a spirit from start to finish, I'd say I'm nowhere near done. I'm going to keep kicking on eternally. From the point where I found myself after death, to learning how to communicate with my mom, to starting the blog, to learning how to be a spirit guide, I was true to myself in allowing myself to be me—nobody greater and nobody less. Through that truth, I found myself.

My mom got a lot out of this experience too. She got the understanding that the world beyond where she's living is real and tangible. She knows I'm always going to be here. She also knows that when she leaves this world, she'll be embraced and loved unconditionally. The new knowledge belongs to her, and that ownership has changed the way she sees and loves me, herself, our relationship, and other people.

Even though dreams and goals are human concepts, I'll try to explain mine in those terms. I will continue to be myself and help people on

Earth remember who they are, where they came from, and what their capabilities are. It's my hope that you will look beyond the entertainment value of this book and be able to say, "Holy shit, dude, this might be real." Even if you don't, though, I hope you've learned something positive from my story. That's the real point. I'd also like you to see that death is not the end. It's a transition. And that anytime you want to, you can reach out to us and we'll be waiting here, ready to guide you when you're ready to open your hearts to us.

So many people ask how the world can be changed, and before I can answer that, I want you to remember that from our perspective, there is no better or worse. There are only lessons. The "struggles" and "suffering" you think humanity has to go through gives you those lessons, and lessons help humanity grow. But looking at it from your perspective—which is what I have to do to help you understand—making the world a "better" place involves first and foremost loving yourself.

So yeah, take care of yourself, man. Some people might take that bit of advice to mean "be selfish." Nah, they've got it all wrong. How can you love anyone else or do any good in the world if you don't at least like yourself first? Learn how to really appreciate and love yourself, and when you do that shit, your light shines on everyone around you. I couldn't figure out how to make that work when I was alive, but I see it now, so clearly. If I could pick one parting message for this book, it'd be that. No matter how tough life gets and how shitty you feel sometimes, know that reaching out, empathizing, and spreading understanding and love is always gonna be the way forward.

Being emotionally honest with other people can also change the world for the "better," not just on the individual level, because, along with being emotionally honest with yourself, you become your truest self in the process, and that shit ripples out across the globe, one person at a time. I guess in a "better world," it would be less a matter of focusing on stamping out the darkness in the world and more of letting more light in. In order to start those ripples flowing, though, love should always be a priority. You have to feel that down to your bones. Once you figure that out, love will give things value, and that's what makes gratitude. Be grateful for everything in your life that's valuable—and everything is.

The last thing that I think would help make the world a "better" place is to realize that everything has a collective life force—even the Earth—and that means there is no separation. Separation is an illusion. We're all part of a whole, and in this unity, we find and spread love.

I won't end with a fanfare. No drumroll. No fireworks. I'll just end with, "See you later."

Afterword

....

by Jamie Butler
(Erik's Spirit Translator)

Meeting Erik Medhus for the first time was a shock. I was on vacation with my family in Florida, staying at my parents' house. When I do any channeling work there I have to hide in my parents' guest bedroom to find quiet and privacy. I sit on the floor and wedge my feet on the wall with my back pushed up against the side of the queen-size bed. Once the call began, I was immediately confronted with Erik's candid and raw experience of his death. Without warning, I began to cry.

I don't normally cry in sessions, but there are times when a spirit like Erik is able to transport you and reenact the scene—the time and place where their tragedy happened. Without the power to do anything but observe, I felt incredibly helpless. Here I was, able to see every detail of Erik's suicide and death, with his mother on the other end of the phone line who could not. Erik shared every detail with me by showing what he had seen along with having me feel what he had felt. It was intense and visceral. I could see and feel Erik sitting at his desk, the cold steel of the gun in his hand, his calm face . . . the shot.

Erik's willingness to talk to his mother, Elisa, about every detail of his death was emotionally raw. At first Erik's spirit sat in front of me, but as he got into his story, he would pace the room back and forth. He was calm and gentle to his mother. But out of his calm would come the harshest words, and it was such a contradiction that I often did not know how to react to him.

In my career as a medium, I have worked with spirits and deaths of all kinds, but never one like Erik. He did not guide himself with any kind of social mores or manners. Erik did not play by those rules. If he knew I was going to be uncomfortable or shocked, he would not stop but forge on. I would not say he does this just for the shock factor or to stand out. He always had a tone in his voice that was ever reminding me to just get over it! I had to face the fact that it was more my problem, my embarrassments and hang-ups. Erik has taught me that "a word is a word is a word. It is the intent behind the word that holds the energy to it." And for Erik, his cussing and harsh language only holds his intent to be honest and real—to be nothing but himself.

During this first session, Erik's colorful words made me wonder if I was hearing him correctly, but Elisa asked me to repeat exactly every single word her son was saying. She explained to me that this was the way he talked when he was living, and Erik told me this is the way he talks when he is dead. All I could do was accept this and go along to the end.

After the session, Erik and Elisa's story weighed heavily on me for days. Erik's images of his suicide were stuck in my head. Erik had extreme bipolar disorder, and he was able to show and have me feel how he struggled with it—the kind of confusion, depression, and pain you can't put words to. I had not experienced mental illness like this before. Elisa seemed to understand her son so well. She had such forgiveness and undying love for him in our session, and she understood his bipolar challenges. She was a very present mother with him, but I could see that there was a divide, a cavern of black space between them:

Erik saying he was with her always and Elisa seeing her son as dead and gone. She knew the channeled conversation we had was real, but she had no way of bringing the experience over into her everyday life that was filled with grief and loss. You could hear her lose her son all over again when she said good-bye and hung up the phone.

I wanted to help Elisa understand that there is no true separation, but the call was over and my job was done. I had to accept that I had done my best work and to let go. I sat in the guest bedroom and sobbed. Eventually, I stood up, acted like this was any other day, and put a smile on for my kids as I walked out of the room.

Soon after, Elisa scheduled more sessions to speak with Erik, and my relationship with Elisa and Erik grew quickly. Elisa found a new comfort in our sessions, or what we prefer to call conversations, as she started to ask questions not just about Erik but also about the afterlife and spirit world. These conversations were exciting! Eventually Elisa asked if she could post these conversations with Erik on her blog, *Channeling Erik*. I agreed. I could not think of a better way for this mother and son duo to show their love and openness for each other.

The blog turned into this amazing journey of discovery about life, death, and the afterlife. Through the combination of Elisa's endless curiosity, diverse questions from her blog readers, and Erik's firsthand answers, the blog unexpectedly became a much bigger conversation with a community of afterlife explorers. Most of these conversations, and Elisa's journey from skeptic to believer, became the material for the first book, *My Son and the Afterlife* (2013). When Elisa asked me to participate as Erik's medium and spirit translator for the second book, I was on board before she finished the question.

I remember that during these new series of sessions, Erik would show up at my office ten to fifteen minutes before his mom would call in. There were plenty of times when he came in early just to prank me. (If you don't know this yet, Erik has a very unique sense of humor and loves to play pranks.) I have had my computer turn on and off and open programs I was not running, or my iTunes would open up and play selected music. My cell phone even turned on a few times by itself.

I have learned to ask Erik before the session to please not mess with the equipment. He normally just gives me a cute smile and shakes his head of messy hair, reminding me that it's okay to lighten up and laugh a little. When my office phone rings, he shouts, "It's my mom!" Then Erik sits on the back of my chair or on the couch with his feet on the cushion to do his confessional-style sharing. Erik shares his heart with his mom in each conversation. Sometimes it is so personal I feel like I should get up and leave them alone.

Sometimes when I hear Erik give messages to me with his causal matter-of-fact talk and goofy gestures, I think he doesn't care. I get frustrated with him for not treating topics such as grief, death, or pain gently. But this is far from Erik's truth. He is a hardworking, compassionate, and loving spirit spending his time changing the world's viewpoint with the blog and conversations as well as offering the much-needed healing that comes from humor and laughter with the occasional prank and joke.

Five years since that first phone call and session, Erik has become a friend, a brother, and a mentor to me. He is a loving spirit guide, so authentic and personable. Erik has such an impact on people, and I am so blessed to help Erik have a bigger voice. I am so glad you are a part of his journey. And if I know Erik, he now considers you a part of his family, and this means you are in line to get pranked. Don't say I didn't warn you!

Acknowledgments

··

I have so much to say to those who have supported me through the process of writing this book, but it's more than just gratitude that I feel. It's love. How can gratitude describe the hand-holding it took to help me through this emotional journey, the pain I felt when revisiting the tragedy, and the tears I often failed to hold back. At those times when I was at my weakest, I asked myself if it was worth it to continue writing, but then I remembered who I was doing this for: my son. I have all of you to thank for helping me find the strength to go on, strength I never knew I had.

First, I appreciate my exceptionally talented editors, Emily Han, Sylvia Spratt, Lindsay Brown, and Henry Covey. They always know how to chip the rock from a freshly mined opal and polish it to a glossy sheen. Not only that, but they also put up with Erik's grammar, rambling, and sailor talk with grace (along with the occasional grimace, I'm sure).

To Richard Cohn, publisher of Beyond Words, thank you for entrusting me to do justice to Erik's memoir. I'm also grateful for Judith Curr, the head honcho at Atria, for giving us the green light to proceed.

Next, I thank my literary agent, Rita Rosenkranz, without whom this book would not have been possible. (Erik would have haunted her if she had not suggested to Beyond Words Publishing the possibility of a follow-up book to *My Son and the Afterlife*.)

I have so much love and gratitude for Erik's spirit translator, Jamie Butler. Jamie, Jamie, Jamie, it's beyond belief how gracefully you put up with Erik's pranks, cursing, and bluntness. Few would have been able to. Thank you for giving my son back to me.

I'm also grateful to you, Maria. You helped me raise my children and put up with their boundless energy and their mischievous naughtiness. From the time that he was eighteen months old up until his death, you gave Erik many of his happiest days. It took unimaginable courage for you to be the first one to open his door and see him after his short life had ended. Many would have walked away and never come back, but you still stand with us through thick and thin. I'm honored to call you part of my family. I'm honored to call you my friend.

Robert, I love you, and I'm so glad you're my friend and Erik's too. Not only have you helped me connect to my own heart but you've also helped me connect to Erik, thanks to your gifts as a spirit translator.

Aunt Teri, you're a rock, because while you were with our family during that dreadful day and helped us get through the horror and sadness, you kept a cool head—cool enough to help us with the arrangements and other tasks that we didn't have the strength and mind-set to do. I guess that comes from being the bossy big sister.

Aunt Laura and Uncle Jim, I adore you both. During the months and years that followed Erik's death, you were there for my family and me and provided us with the emotional support we needed to go on. Not only are you family but you're also our friends. Plus, you snuck smokes to Erik from time to time, and, oh, how he loved that!

There are not enough words to express how deeply I love my other children, Kristina, Michelle, Lukas, and Annika. Your strength was the light that guided me through that dark forest of grief—not an easy task as you struggled with your own grief over the death of your brother. Remember, though, he's not gone. He's still around to pester, annoy, and love you if you open your minds and hearts to receive him.

Rune, my soul mate, despite the tragic story that is now ours to bear forever, yours is the strength that gives me something to lean on during my darkest days. I love you.

Lastly, Erik. My dear son, you transformed your untimely death into something beautiful, and now you're helping (and pranking) people all over the world. I couldn't be prouder. Only in death did you truly find yourself. Only in death did you come to life. I miss you. I miss the hugs and kisses. I miss fussing at you to do your chores or homework. I miss calling you downstairs for dinner. I miss kissing you good-bye and telling you to be careful when you're about to drive to school or to a friend's house. I still go through some hard days of grief sometimes, but I'm happy for you. I really am. I love you, sweetie, and I always will.

Discussion and
Reading Group Questions

1. Before reading this book, what were your thoughts about your own death? How about the afterlife?
2. Do you consider yourself a skeptic of or a believer in an afterlife? Why?
3. Do you fear death? If so, has this book changed those fears? How?
4. Do you believe in a heaven? If so, how has this book changed your thoughts about heaven?
5. Erik's role in heaven is a spirit guide. As a spirit, what role would you want to have?
6. What are your thoughts about Erik's description of his life review in chapter 5?
7. Have you had any forms of communication with Erik, including pranks and visits?
8. Can you think of a time when you experienced a loved one communicating with you?
9. How do you connect to Erik and his story and experience?

10. If you read *My Son and the Afterlife*, how does this book continue the personal stories of Erik and Elisa Medhus?

11. Have you read any other books on the same subject matter? If so, how is this book similar and different?

12. If you mourn the loss of a loved one, has this book helped you through your grieving process?

13. What do you think Erik's main messages are?

14. What other questions do you have about death and the afterlife that have not been answered?

15. After reading this book, have your beliefs changed about death? About the afterlife?

Recommended Resources

The following resources are just a few of many and should serve as a supplement to the support of family members, friends, and mental healthcare providers.

Suicide Prevention

If suicide is imminent, please call 911.

National Suicide Prevention Lifeline: (800) 273-TALK (8255):
  www.suicidepreventionlifeline.org
Suicide Awareness Voices of Education (SAVE): (800) 273-8255:
  www.save.org
RemedyLIVE (a place to chat anonymously): www.remedylive.com
Your Life, Your Voice: (800) 448-3000; www.yourlifeyourvoice.org

Depression and Bipolar Disorder

DailyStrength Bipolar Disorder Support Group: www.dailystrength
  .org/c/Bipolar-Disorder/support-group
Depression and Bipolar Support Alliance: www.dbsalliance.org
National Institute of Mental Health (NIMH): www.nimh.nih.gov

Mental Illness in General

NAMI.org features the latest information on mental health illnesses, medication, and treatment and resources for support and advocacy. NAMI offers various support and services such as:

- The NAMI helpline: (800) 950-NAMI (6264)
- NAMI Basics: a free educational program for parents and other primary caregivers of children and adolescents living with mental illness.
- NAMI Connection: a recovery support group for adults living with mental illness regardless of their diagnosis. Every group meeting is offered free of charge and meets weekly for 90 minutes.
- NAMI Family-to-Family: a free twelve-week course for family caregivers of adults living with mental illness.
- NAMI Hearts and Minds: an online interactive wellness educational initiative intended to promote quality of life and recovery for individuals who live with mental illness.
- NAMI Peer-to-Peer: a ten-week education course on the topic of recovery for any person living with a serious mental illness.

StrengthofUs is an online social community for teens and young adults living with mental illness: www.strengthofus.org

Bereavement

Bereaved Parents
The Compassionate Friends: www.compassionatefriends.org
Bereaved Parents of the USA: www.bereavedparentsusa.org
M.E.N.D. (Mommies Enduring Neonatal Death): www.mend.org
National Organization of Parents of Murdered Children:
    www.pomc.com
Peace After Abortion: www.peaceafterabortion.com

Bereaved Children
The Compassionate Friends: www.compassionatefriends.org
The Dougy Center, the National Center for Grieving Children and
    Families: www.dougy.org
National Alliance for Grieving Children:
    www.nationalallianceforgrievingchildren.org

Bereaved Families
Family Lives On Foundation: www.familyliveson.org

Bereaved Spouses and Partners
Legacy Connect: www.connect.legacy.com
Surviving Spouses Support Group: www.survivingspousesupport
    group.org

Support for Those Who Mourn a Victim of Cancer
CancerCare: www.cancercare.org

Bereaved Pet Owners
Association for Pet Loss and Bereavement: www.aplb.org
Pet Partners: www.petpartners.org

Bereaved Twins
Twinless Twins Support Group, Intl.: www.twinlesstwins.org